The Author

Since reading *Memories, Dreams, and Reflections* by C.G Jung in her teens, Mariana Funes knew that she wanted to dedicate her life to the study of mind. A first degree in Psychology from Warwick University followed by an M.Sc. in Intelligent Systems, and a PhD Knowledge Acquisition for Expert Systems have given her a sound base for a long career as an Executive Cognitive Coach. She is an author, a chartered psychologist, and fellow at the Royal Society of Arts. She has always tried to push the boundaries of conventional wisdom in business: highlighting the human side of knowledge management in her first book, using laughter as a tool for creative living in her second and now challenging clock time as a time management technique in *Lived Time*.

As a result of writing and applying the techniques in *Lived Time*, she finds herself leading a contemplative life whilst she continues to write, run her cognitive coaching business on a donation only basis and continue to run her organizational consulting and e-learning business along more traditional business lines. She is currently on a supervised 3 year and 1 month part time retreat in the Thai Theravada Buddhist Tradition, to support a contemplative life in a hectic world. Her previous publications include: *Honing Your Knowledge Skills*, and *Laughing Matters: How to live creatively with laughter*. She is at peace with life and has all the time in the world to do what she loves – be of service to others and walk her dog Colin, a little Jack Russell that has changed her life.

If you want to contact her with experiences, questions or ideas, please do so at www.marianafunes.co.uk.

Quotes and Testimonials

"Your beautiful and important book deserves to be published, it has changed my life and I continue to use it to find more lived time in my life. How wonderful for us all that your wisdom can be in our hands soon."
Nancy Kline, author of 'Time to think' and 'More Time to Think', USA

"The biggest issue that leaders in my organisation have is time. Mariana takes a new look at this issue and will help everyone who has the patience and belief to look at time in a much more holistic way. Mariana says, 'Just change the way you think.' If you can do that – and this book shows you how – the world will open up."
Brian Chernett, Founder of The Academy for Chief Executives and Chief Executive of the ELLA FOUNDATION, UK

"This manuscript definitely deserves to become a book. I was really inspired reading the text, and feel sure it will benefit many people."
Gill Farrer-Halls, freelance editor, UK.

LIVED TIME

Life beyond clock time

Mariana Funes

*For a complete list of Management Books 2000 titles
visit our web-site on http://www.mb2000.com*

Copyright © Mariana Funes 2012

Illustrations by Danny Burgess

All rights reserved. No part of this publication may be reproduced, stored in a retrieval system, or transmitted in any form or by any means, electronic, mechanical, photocopying, recording, or otherwise without the prior permission of the publishers.

First published in 2012 by Management Books 2000 Ltd
36 Western Road
Oxford Ox1 4LG
United Kingdom
Tel: 0044 (0) 1865 600738
Web: www.mb2000.com

This book is sold subject to the condition that it shall not, by way of trade or otherwise, be lent, resold, hired out, or otherwise circulated without the publisher's prior consent in any form of binding or cover other than that in which it is published and without a similar condition including this condition being imposed upon the subsequent purchaser.

British Library Cataloguing in Publication Data is available

ISBN 9781852526542

Life was never meant to be a struggle
Just a gentle progression
From one point to another,
Much like walking through a valley
On a sunny day
S.Wilde

I dedicate this book to the people in my life who help me each day to see life as a walk through a valley on a sunny day. I hope I have done justice to our conversations in the words that follow.

CONTENTS

Introduction 9
Clock time 21
   Living in clock time 25
   The business of busyness 32
   The diseases of clock time 36
   A principle too far? 43

A faulty sense of time 45
   The price we pay for living in clock time 48
   Defining success in clock time 65
   The signs of a faulty sense of time 68

Lived time 83
   Types of time 86
   Understanding lived time 89

Making the most of time 107
   There <u>really</u> aren't enough hours in the day 108
   Developing a healthy sense of time 112
   Meditations in time 114
   A living Present: On the art and science of attention 117
   A life with a healthy sense of time – David 145
   A few more stepping stones to a healthy sense of time 154

A philosophy of time 157
   The re-unification of time and body 167
   Growth is more than just 'more-thinking' 176
   'Measuring' quality 179
   Reversing conventional wisdom – a way to lived time 185
   And in conclusion – Just stop 187
   A summary of the book 190

Appendix. A Meditation practice to find time *by Rev. Andrew Hunter* 193

Bibliography 199

INTRODUCTION

'The reality is that our minds, our attention, our abilities of mental perception are embedded in our lives. In the type of mental activities we engage in, the types of emotions we foster, the type of physical activities we engage in...and so the Buddha's practice starts with: 'Look at the way you are living!!''
Alan Wallace[1]

Why does time management not work? Because we do not want to take a look at the way we are living. Only continue reading if you are willing to take a look.

I am not aiming to make this book an easy or a fast read. I am not interested in offering 'quick fixes' to squeeze a few more activities into your day. I am interested in exploring the connection between the way we live our lives and the way we relate to time. Many approaches to managing time assume it is possible to look at skill development in isolation. My approach suggests that time cannot be managed, and that our relationship to time has to be looked at as part of the overall picture of how we choose to live our lives. This book is not about putting a plaster on a cut that keeps bleeding; it is about finding out what is getting us hurt in the first place, so that we can do without plasters altogether. I have not written a well signposted journey to THE ANSWER – I ask that you have the willingness and the courage to look for the cause rather than keep fixing the effect. I assume that you may have picked up this book because fixing the effect is not working

---

[1]   2001, York, UK, From 'Beyond the Brain' Conference held every 2 years by the Scientific and Medical Network. Info@scimednet.org.

for you anymore. We don't need to learn to manage time in order to live well, but we do need to live well in order to have all the time in the world.

My intention in this book is to holistically explore body, mind and spirit at work. I will look at the whole of life not just the workplace, but it is in the workplace that I spend my days. What has informed my ideas above all has been the many formal and informal conversations with the managers, directors and chief executives I work with every day in my capacity as a consultant psychologist to large organisations. I coach, I teach, I facilitate and I listen.

The book started with an idea I had about my work: perhaps the greatest contribution I make to those I consult with is time. Whatever our topic – communication, difficult people or basic management skills – I started to believe that the formal structures I offered were giving people time to think, reflect and re-connect with the wisdom of their own sense of time. Once the space was held, within the structure of a workshop for example, people got a clear view of what they needed to do, or say, to solve their own problems when they got back to work. Maybe I was just selling time. I started my research and these pages are the result.

I started teaching management as an 'odd job' when I was studying for my PhD in cognitive psychology, 22 years ago. Although I had had a 'real' job in the private sector for a number of years before returning to university, I was an academic with every intention of continuing on the academic path once I completed my doctorate. However, during this time, I was asked to run assertiveness training programmes for some managers in an IT organisation. I was dismissive of the project and of anybody who dared suggest that it might be interesting. Even in those days I was grappling with my own relationship to time, although I was not aware of it; I was trying to complete a doctorate, run a software development business and also teach at the university. But the money was good so I ran assertiveness training courses. It was my first lesson in humility.

I discovered that working in the business world with real people, grappling with real problems, gave me a degree of satisfaction I had only experienced when sitting in front of my computer writing or programming. I started to make comparisons between the academic world I was part of and the business world I was starting to learn about. After my initial introduction to management training, I realised there was a complex network of relationships playing out in each department of every organisation I had ever been in. Years have gone by and I have worked with so many different organisations around the world, listening to them grapple with one basic question: what does it mean to work well? I cannot be grateful enough to each and every one of those people for helping me form the views that I present in this book. If any of it is useful it will be thanks to their willingness to share their problems with me and experiment with the ideas I present to them through my work.

So there is a method to the madness that follows. I have spoken to many, researched much and then put it all together in my very own subjective and idiosyncratic way. I hope that the book you hold in your hands will bring you many inefficient hours of slow reading. Before finding a home with its publishers this book lived with me for several years. I have loved it, I have hated it, I have bored many people with the ideas in its pages and I have been blessed with many great conversations about its content.

In writing this book I have an agenda. I am offering a point of view and I am rejecting another. Those of us who work in the area of management generally, and work-life balance specifically, tend to assume that work pressures are a given, that we have to learn to hold the tension that inevitably exists between living well and working well. We believe that the pressures of the modern workplace are a given, and that all that we can do is learn how to manage them. I create an image of this view where the employee holds a pair of scales; work on one side and life on the other. Their never-ending, and excruciatingly painful, job is to keep the balance between the two sides. Add more work here, take a bit of life from there. A bit of life here, well then we must take away work from there. Work, life, work, life, but you never quite find a resolution to the tension between the two. This is the view I am rejecting. Many organisational initiatives help the employee maintain a precarious balance. But, I believe that there is more to life than a struggle for balance. If all you want are more techniques to help you keep or regain the balance between work and life, these pages are not for you.

The years I have spent teaching these techniques have convinced me that there is another way. For a long time I did not know what that other way was. Now I do, and that is the view I offer in this book. If you have ever asked yourself the question – what if there was a way of resolving this constant tension? Then keep reading. I am offering the view that it is possible, once and for all, to let go of the pressure of not having enough time to get everything done. So, if you are after disembodied, surgical techniques that provide yet more ways to do more with less, look elsewhere. If you want to re-think the issue of time altogether, by taking time to think about time, then do keep reading.

Since Alec Mackenzie coined the term 'time management' in the 1960's many people have written on the subject.[2] Time management books follow a predictable path starting with philosophical quotations about time and moving on to tell us how to manage 'it': priority setting, task definition, delegation, etc. In the beginning time management was presented as a way of managing stress, nowadays books have a more spiritual flavour. Most approaches still assume that it is we who are unable to manage time, or who do not know how to divide it up effectively.

In essence, approaches to time management are locked into a rational clock-time view. These approaches promise that we can affect our future through rational control. This illusion of control has become an addiction at work and, increasingly, in the rest of our lives. We are clock time addicts. We complain about lack of time and yet find ourselves unable to change our way of life. This book explores possible reasons for our inability to apply what we know about time management to help us run our life at our own pace. It takes on the challenge of finding a more holistic view of time. Sabelis asks us to look beyond a reductionistic view of time: 'If the image of manageable time persists, the social necessity of surrendering and adapting to that image will not be far off.' I believe that we have already surrendered. The literature leaves us believing that there is

---

[2] For example, Ida Sabelis 'Time management: Paradoxes and patterns'. This paper has a review of time management approaches over the past 20 years, the conclusions that follow are summarised from this article. *Time and Society*, Vol. 10 (2/3), pp. 387-400.

a best way, that this best way is clock time and that we can take or leave that best way. If we take it, we are effective and successful. If we don't, we are said to be ineffective or to be making a lifestyle choice; the meaning of these two terms often blurred in the minds of those we work with.

It is true that there are not enough hours in the day to do all of the things we set out to do. I will argue that the cause for our stated lack of time is not a lack of knowledge or skills, but a lack of a sense of time. We have become disconnected from the richness of time as our senses experience it. We live in a society that treats time as money and believes that time lives outside of us and needs to be controlled. We rush more and more to get to a place where we can stop, but we keep on rushing because at an existential level we do not want to stop. We are too disconnected from the stability of our past and too afraid of the future to take our focus away from rushing in the present. We have come to think of our present as a 'things to do today' list. We use our lives outside of work as a cushion for unexpected disturbance at work, and think that this is the only way to be.

What if we were to relearn the richness of time as embedded in action rather than disembodied from it? We might then be willing to sit with the distress of our fears for the future, find ways of refocusing on what is stable in our lives and find a frame of reference that is grounded in something other than 'me' as the centre of the world. There is no magic formula that allows us to continue on the path to self-serving goals and also find time to live. We can explore a new path, one where we learn to live 'in' time. We might then find ourselves re-discovering a sense of being part of a world that can support us, rather than making us feel dysfunctional and in need of self-help or personal development.

If we agree to bring time back to live 'in' us rather than outside of us, we might discover that there is no rush, that we can find release from that constant inner chatter and that we can have peace of mind today. But, there is a price to pay for this sense of being at peace with a living present. It is not true that we can have it all – time and being the top employee, a quiet life and a directorship. Those who tell us that we can are selling a political message that continues to keep us compliant and forever trying to fix ourselves. We then have no free attention left to notice that it is our energy and well being that is being sapped in the service of an ever shorter and shallower Now. Some researchers tell us that the workplace is changing, and that we are no longer considered weak if we cannot keep up with the pace of our workplaces. We hear that companies are keen to keep employees and to reduce absences due to stress.[3] Yet my day-to-day conversations with those I work with paint a picture that is in stark contrast with this view.

Measures are being taken at the physical level and at the level of employees taking time out to be ready to get back into the ring. What is never questioned is the pace of work itself.[4] This book argues that it is precisely because of the pace that we are prevented from reflecting about our unsustainable lifestyles. Rather than challenging this unsustainable pace, we keep extending the image of time as a manageable resource to more and more of our life outside of work. The end result of this is that we have become guests in our own existence. We are slaves to 'ticktockman' both at work and outside it in order to sustain the unsustainable. Only to the extent that we are willing to reconnect with our sense of embodied time will we truly know that our time is our own, and only then can we regain our freedom from the clock and from a frenetic pace of life. Time is not money but life.

The style of this book is one that meanders through as you might when driving in a little country lane on a sunny day in summer. It takes its time, it goes around in circles to explore meanings and ideas, and slowly arrives at new concepts and definitions.

This style is different from the way most books on time management are written nowadays. We have so unquestioningly accepted the metaphor 'time is money' that we often feel that meandering is a 'waste of time'. We have the new trend of 'little books' on big subjects. These create the illusion that it is possible to know about, say, relationships by reading a few hundred words. We

---
[3] Ibid. Page 393. I read many messages like this in the literature, I see little of the practice in my experience of organisational life.

[4] Ibid. page 393. The pace is a given. Employees have to develop the competency to handle the pace or they can be labelled 'personally inadequate'. The fact that one could challenge the sustainability of the pace itself, is not part of the argument.

also have books that promise 10 or 6 or 7 easy steps to effectiveness of one kind or another. The ethos of these books has its roots in what David Bohm refers to as 'discussion'. He points out that the word 'discussion' has the same root as 'percussion' and 'concussion', and really means to break things up. It emphasises the idea of analysis – analysing and breaking up. By breaking up human activity into easily digestible chunks we gain ease, but we lose authenticity. We gain efficiency and lose our humanity. The economist Edward Luttwak says: 'Whatever is worthwhile about us, as individuals, groups and societies is the inefficient part. Inefficiency is where human life exists, social life exists, where love, hatred and culture exist.'

Luttwak believes that: 'efficiency in business should be presumed bad until it can be proved good'.[5] This is certainly a controversial view, and in daring to attack our efficiency god, he has written a book that provides an in-depth economic rationale for this view. The book warns us against believing that time is money, and points out that by pursuing efficiency we are becoming poor people with money. We have only money, nothing else. This then means that we must defend money at all costs, which keeps leading us to take the easy route to preserve it, irrespective of the cost to the world and our future.

I don't want you to suffer 'concussion' by reading an efficient book. I suggest we go where human life exists and dare to be inefficient! This goes against the flow of books that teach us how to break up time into smaller and smaller units in order to become more and more efficient and less and less human. This book asks you to engage with the messy and complex business of finding your own answer to the question: 'What is my relationship to time?' I want you to get to the last page feeling that you have all the time in the world. My wish is that you never again find yourself saying the dreary words: 'I would love to, but I haven't got time', or 'there just aren't enough hours in the day!'

This is a lofty aim, but it has no objectives. I do not offer you a magic recipe to manage your time – 'the 6 even easier steps to perfect time management'. I do not offer a solution to a problem – 'how to have

---

[5] *Turbo-Capitalism: Winners and Losers in the Global Economy* by E Luttwak, 1999. Harper-Collins.

all the time in the world without changing anything in your life', or a cure for a disease – 'a cure for clock time addiction'. In early drafts of this book I did go down the cure route. I thought I could find the 12-step approach to becoming a recovering time addict. I will discuss clock time addiction, but I do not have 'The Cure'. Our notion of how we use time cannot be separated from the notion of how we choose to live our lives. In a very real sense all we have is time. Did you know that we have on average 30,000 days to live? Is our aim in life to live most of those days being at peace with ourselves, or is our aim to spend most of those days chasing the few thousand that might (yes, only might) be left at the end to find some peace? These are very difficult questions to ask ourselves. It is much easier to be distracted by the clock and focus on how we cannot put anymore into our days. I suggest that you only ask these difficult questions if your aim is to have peace of mind today, rather than in an uncertain future.

This book is about how we work, but most of all it is about how we live. It is easy for those of us who work as the 'effectiveness gurus' of the business world to keep telling you how to live. If you learn this particular set of steps, if you become something other than who you are, if you change your approach to your work environment in this particular way then you will be in control of your life. The approach offered here is not so easy.

Until I started to ask myself the seemingly obvious question 'What is time?' I believed that these tools and techniques were 'The Cure', and that if my work-life balance was not what I wanted it to be, then it was because there was something else that I had not yet become, as Krishnamurti tells us. Human beings took a wrong turn when we internalised the notion of clock time in our concept of always being on the way to somewhere – always on the way to become something else. It is this false concept that leads us to be in constant conflict with who we are right now. Nowhere is this clearer than in the underlying assumptions of people working in organisational development. A colleague of mine summarised this well: 'you can change somebody into anything, the only question is do you have enough time and money to do it?' In this field we certainly reject Picasso's assertion: 'I don't develop, I am'.

I believe in the good intentions embedded in my field of work –

we do want to support people in organisations to be effective – but I question that this can best be done by using a method that simplifies the complexities of being human into easy recipes for 'Unlimited Power at Work'. I also question the implicit assumption that if my clients are not able to make my easy recipe work it is somehow their fault. We would never say that, of course; we would just say that maybe they are not yet at a place in their life where they can make it work. Maybe it does not matter who is at fault. Is our work more pastoral than it is developmental? I wonder if where we are of most value is in the care we offer our clients rather than in our easy recipes.

It is not a universal truth that time exists in the objective sense we attach to it when we manage clock time and our work schedules. In managing clock time we have not found ourselves in control of our working lives and with all the time in the world. Quite the opposite is true. Every other conversation I have with people in the workplace is about how they will get their life under control in the future, but how their lives are running away with them today. The popularity of work-life initiatives and research within the field may be a symptom of how desperate we all are to find a way to stop feeling that our life is not our own.

If we have reached the limit of what we can do with clock time, maybe it is time to take time to think about time! What is it that keeps us trying harder and harder to manage time in smaller and smaller chunks? What is it that keeps us creating only small islands of slow time in a vast sea of frenetic speed and out-of-control living, even when we know better? What keeps us having a lifestyle in which we forget the last time we had a holiday? What is it that makes me not want to confess to my colleagues that my time is running at just the right speed for me? What is it that makes us engage in the basic conversational script of 'my-time-is-more scarce-than-yours' several times a day?

I think that part of the answer is encapsulated in the following story. I attended a conference recently and decided to participate in a workshop on work-life balance. The person running it asked his audience of about 50 people: 'How many of you feel that you have the right balance between your work and the rest of your life?' After a long pause in which nobody raised their hand, one person reluctantly and apologetically raised her hand half way. The room burst out laughing. The conversation that ensued had the effect of making this person feel ashamed that her life was her own, and that the reason for this must be either that she was deluding herself or that her work did not have enough responsibility. We have a lot invested in keeping our lives out of balance.

We say we want time, but our actions are not congruent with this desire. In her book 'The Time Bind' Arlie Hochschild shows substantial evidence to support her thesis that work-life initiatives are actually not being taken up by workers because the long hours are effectively being used as an excuse for not exploring the disconnection that is felt within family life. She says that most families are engaging in relational loafing in front of the TV. She argues that human beings are losing the skill of working with the discomfort and messiness of real life. We are becoming a society allergic to the messiness of real life. As the character Carrie says in a 'Sex in the City' episode: 'Reality? Yuck!' – in response to looking at a picture of herself without make-up. These two words encapsulate a trend that characterises our lives and interactions more and more. We have become victims of comfort. As David Whiteland says: 'You should never underestimate the power of comfort. To our everlasting discredit, we owe our utter dependency on technology to our inability to resist it.'[6] As one of my favourite songs says, it may just be too late for us victims of comfort.[7]

Hochschild's research points to a simple but tough reality in our relationship to time, that the reification of time is a convenient way to hide from our conscious awareness, from our felt lack of connection with the people in our work and our lives each day. We wish for time in the future, and use our time today to insulate ourselves from reality. At work we have created the appearance of real relationships, but we relate to each other only in carefully scripted ways. Those who initially choose not to are 'sent' on training programmes where they learn the secret language of 'effective communication'. When they go back to work, they follow the new rules of communication if they

---

[6] The book of pages, 2000. See www.bookofpages.com.
[7] From song by Keb' Mo'. From Album by the same name. Release Date: Jun 7, 1994. www.kebmo.com Track listing for CD (EK 057863).

want to go up the promotion ladder. I should know, I teach the secret language.

It is in this sense that we have become clock time addicts. We are using time as a drug to help us avoid facing the tragic consequences of having created an efficient world. In losing the inefficiency we are losing our humanness. It is more comfortable to talk about how little time we have, and turn this into a measure of how important we are, than to stop and really attend to the habits of body, speech and mind that create the quality of life that we have today.

My whole life has been a journey to a life beyond clock time. It has not been a straight road; it has been a windy road full of episodes of feeling in control and out of control at different times of each year. Today I feel more often in control than out of control. Along the way I have had to compose a life that honours my inner sense of time, and is independent of the frenetic pace of life around me. It has been hard to get here, and I still pay a price for the choices I make daily. What have I gained? I have a sense of being at peace with the world and myself most of the time. I have the freedom to pursue my dreams, and the privilege of being surrounded by people in my life who take the time to care and listen. What I need each day is the courage to keep my own time when all around me is saying 'faster, faster, faster'.

The pages that follow will tackle these issues in a messy and human way. I want you, the reader, to feel challenged, stimulated, and motivated to question your relationship to time. I want you to develop your inner sense of lived time. I believe that if we look at the search for work-life balance as a symptom of faulty time perception, then it becomes possible to develop new ways of perceiving time, and thus to find new ways of working and living. We can develop a relationship to time that may bring us the quality of life we want in a living present rather than a disconnected future. For this to happen we do not need to learn any techniques, but we do need to stop and ask some difficult questions about how we choose to live today and why.

What kind of a self-help book is this that offers no easy answers, no quick answers? Read on.

CLOCK TIME

Lived Time

> *Sometimes I wonder, could I get to a position where all my time is spent managing my time? I am always surprised at the amount of time I spend looking at my diary, and thinking about time.*
> An interviewee[8]

What is your lived experience of time? People have a love-hate relationship to it and seldom feel that time is on their side. Here is a not-so-random sample of what they say:

- I don't know where the time goes
- Life is changing so fast, I am constantly running to keep up
- The more I do the more there is to be done
- Have you got a window in the next couple of months?
- This year I will take more time for myself, I said that last year!
- It takes me at least a week to slow down when I go on holidays
- If the holiday is too long I get restless
- I am doing so much because I don't want to miss out on anything

Here is an example from my own life. I phoned a friend today after many attempts to organise a birthday outing for us on email. She answered the phone, sounding out of breath and said: 'I'm in the middle of a riding lesson, can I call you back?' A little time later she calls, still out of breath: 'I'm on my way home on the bike, talk to me.' I agreed that she would call me once she got home, not wanting to feel responsible for her having an accident. When she called, she could not get the words out fast enough: 'I'm on my way to the shower and then I'm going straight out again'. We spent a few minutes on the reason for the call. I called back with some information 10 minutes later, she had had her shower and was on her way out again. The morning was a typical Saturday morning for her.

---

[8] When I refer to interviewees in the book, I am talking about the many people who have offered their time, formally and informally, to help me research the ideas in the book. I will not attribute my quotes to individuals to preserve confidentiality.

Your response to this kind of episode will help you decide if this book is for you. Keep reading if your life is like that of my friend, but every so often you get the nagging old feeling that tells you in a whisper: 'I want to stop'. If your life is like my friend's and you choose it that way, read elsewhere. And finally, if you would like to know how to get your life to be more and more like that, I encourage you to put this book down and move along the bookshelf to another title. I can almost guarantee that you will find something more appropriate to your purposes elsewhere in the bookshop.

Developing skills to manage time and stress often fail to give results. Skills and behaviours often just become tools to feed an addiction to clock time. You may well have had that start-of-the-year feeling. The feeling that makes you say: 'I will put my life in order this year,' and makes you spend money on some kind of external system to order your life. It feels good, and you feel you are now in control, but it is not long before your are off-the-wagon again, rushing around and promising to slow down after this particularly busy period. I recognised this cycle in myself, but only after I had been through it a few times. I experienced episodic temporality or déjà vu at the beginning of each year! So what were the episodes I kept watching re-runs of?

I rushed around so much that all I ever talked about was time, or the lack of it to be more precise. But I made myself stop. I decided that I would put my quality of life first from now on only to find myself rushing around again months later. Eventually it became clear to me that I was in the grip of clock time addiction. I was hooked on time, but a particularly shallow and superficial version of time that made me compulsively divide up my hour into smaller and smaller segments. The relief I felt for a little time each year was to do with the illusion of being in control.

Yet the relief was only temporary. Creating breadcrumbs of time allowed me to add more and more activities to my to-do-list so I could stop myself temporarily from feeling the pain of the ever-growing gap between me and the 'good life' I said I wanted. Like water crashing down at the bottom of a waterfall, I was in pursuit of having everything. I was going to have everything, I was entitled to have everything. I did not want to compromise.

I believed the 'new deal' that the song 'Quality Time' promised: 'She's got a phone in one hand, a hairbrush in the other and she says, "Life's too short to stay home and be a mother." She says she can have it all 'cause that's The New Deal, so God give her a hand, 'cause she needs one for the wheel.[9]

Yet I had a heavy feeling in my bones. I kept hearing a little voice, sometimes not so little, that told me I might just end up with nothing. I felt that something was not right about the New Deal I had accepted.

Does any of this fit with your lived experience of time? Do you want to stop and take a look at life as it is and not as you should be able to make it if only you were more skilled or improved? Then I think I might have a companion for my journey.

Our first stop is clock time. The stories above illustrate the idea of living in clock time. As a result of clock time we find ourselves aspiring to achieve what is now fashionably called work-life balance. Those who realise their aspirations often choose to move to a totally new environment. Those who realise their aspirations and stay must carefully manage the impact of their choices on those who are still in pursuit of Everything. In the world of work today we value fast over slow, efficiency over exploration, and change over stability. Klaus Schwab once said, praising the nature of the world of work today, this is now a world in which the fast eat slow.

Let me tell you a recent story. I walk into the business school where I teach and I meet one of my colleagues who has just come back from her break. She tells me how busy she is and before I can stop myself, I say: 'I know. I started back 3 days ago and it feels like I have never been away. I'm exhausted'. I found myself lying in order to fit in. I had just come back from my yearly solitary retreat, I was living in my own time not the clock's, and I certainly was not exhausted. We live in a world that assumes that if we are not rushed and out of time, we are not effective or important enough. I betrayed my sense of time in order to feel important. This is what it is like to live in clock time.

I distinguish between clock time and lived time, following Eugene Minkowski, who was as interested as I am in the differences between time as we experience it and the time of clocks. He sees time as being

---

[9] Iris Dement (1995) *Songs of Iris*, ASCAP.

enmeshed in our subjective lived experience, so our emotions and our activities are structured by time. Therefore, time is no more than a: 'synonym of life in the broadest sense of the word'.[10] Time inside ourselves is not a uniform kind of affair. Take a snapshot of someone walking – she does not walk at the same pace at which she breathes. She does not digest that snack she had before she left the house at the same pace at which she notices and makes sense of the trees around her. She is not shedding dead skin cells at the same pace at which ideas are going through her mind. So many different times are being marked simultaneously, and yet she can feel that time has stopped as she walks. This is lived time.

Time outside of ourselves cannot be stopped, and time management books are not about lived time but clock time – years, months, days, hours, minutes, seconds. Our office clocks have pride of place at work. The clock is the only tool for accurately measuring our work lives; the single stable fixture in an ever-changing workplace...or if it isn't, we act as if it were. The clock teaches how best to manage time to help us achieve our life goals. There is obviously some value in this approach, and many activities in the workplace would be impossible without it. The value, however, is limited.

All my clients and colleagues experience life at a frenetic pace, which indicates to me that the value of clock time follows the law of diminishing returns. This means that some systems reach a point in their life cycle where you have to work damn hard to see any result. We experience this when we are learning to play a new sport. We make big leaps in ability early on, but as our proficiency increases we have to practise more and more to get minimal improvement. If we accept the truth of the law of diminishing returns about clock time, then it should make us interested in looking for another way.

Living in clock time

Home is where the food is. He holds a glass of beer and a baguette. He is not drinking from the can but from a glass. He is taking his time

---

[10] E. Minkowski, *Lived Time: phenomenological and psychopathological studies*, translated by N. Metzel, 1933 (page 18). Evanston: Northwest University Press. Quoted in M. Flaherty's *A Watched Pot* (1999).

to eat, unaware that the train is moving at a speed of over 60 miles per hour. The train rattles and shakes, the man holds the glass as if it were crystal not plastic, as if he were at a chic restaurant not on a fast train. He gets up to leave. He wears smart pointy black shoes, the kind every male city dweller seems to be wearing these days. Shoes with that perfectly shiny silver buckle, a steely rectangle in a sea of black. Shoes that perfectly match the perfectly balanced shoulder bags – the bag ladies of the City of London – one shoulder holds the laptop while the other shoulder holds the virtual links with his world, the mobile phone and the smartphone. He carries his home on his shoulder. Home can be a train, a coffee shop, or a waiting room. The dream has come true. Work and live anytime, anyplace, anywhere. With his attention on his virtual world – the office, the meeting he is late for – the debris of his existence is left in the real world. The train stops suddenly and he runs off, leaving behind a can of beer, a crumpled napkin and a dirty plastic glass that will live forever in our real world.

You may recognise yourself in the paragraph above. I wrote it on my smartphone as I observed a man on a train. We live in a culture in which the clock is king, and though we may see the limitations of clock time we cannot always find the courage to look beyond it. Life is not about either clock time or lived time. It is about what psychologist Robert Levine calls multitemporality. It is about understanding what the options are, and then using time in a way that fits with what the situation demands. Life is also about asking some tough questions about concepts that seem irrefutable truths in our lives. The whole area of time management comes from an unquestioned acceptance that time exists outside ourselves and needs to be managed. So, how do we challenge the notion that the only way to live is to manage time and to be driven by our clocks and calendars?

Ralph Keyes wrote a book in 1991 called *Time Lock*. It is now out of print, and I 'wasted' a great deal of time to get my used copy. The book talks about that end-of-the-workday feeling when you disparagingly look at what it was that you didn't get done today before you leave for home. As a colleague once said to me: 'when you consistently end your day with a look at what you did not do today, you start to feel pretty unmotivated about your work'. Or as one of his interviewees phrased it: 'You prioritise, list your musts, and then you cannot even get to your musts'. You are in a state of 'timelock'. Another of his interviewees said: 'time is no longer an issue. There is none'. The idea of timelock regards time as something we can 'have' rather than something we 'are', it is the feeling that we cannot wring even one more second out of our crowded hectic days. Could this describe your experience? To assess the degree to which time pressure affects your life, answer the Timelock questionnaire below. Circle the number that best fits you, even if no single answer feels exactly right. Scoring instructions are given at the end.

1. *In a typical week, how often do you wear or carry a watch?*

    (1) Regularly
    (2) Part of the time
    (3) Occasionally
    (4) Almost never

2. *How many hours do you sleep in an average weeknight?*

    (1) 5 or less
    (2) 6
    (3) 7
    (4) 8 or more

3. *When driving, how often do you exceed the speed limit?*

    (1) Regularly
    (2) Often
    (3) Seldom
    (4) Almost never

4. *As you approach a stoplight while driving, if a green light turns to yellow, are you most likely to:*

    (1) Speed up to get through before it turns to red
    (4) Slow down and wait for the next green light

28   Lived Time

5. Which Statement Best Describes Your Attitude?

   (1) When I have a train or plane to catch, I like to arrive as close as possible to the scheduled departure time so I won't have to waste time sitting around.
   (4) I always try to leave extra time to get to an airport or train station so I won't have to worry about missing a train or flight.

6. (1) I like my food to arrive as soon as possible after I've ordered.
   (4) I don't mind waiting a few minutes for the food I've ordered at a restaurant.

7. (1) What I like about microwave ovens is that they cut down on the amount of time it takes to prepare meals.
   (4) I'd rather spend extra time preparing meals than use a microwave oven on a regular basis.

8. (1) I often use a remote control device to scan a lot of television channels so I can see what's on.
   (4) To me a remote control device is a convenient tool for turning the television on or off from a distance, adjusting the volume, or occasionally changing channels.

9. (1) I like the lively pace of today's television programs.
   (4) I have trouble keeping up with the pace of today's television programmes.

10. (1) With so many other demands on my time, I find it hard to keep up friendships.
    (4) I try to make time to see my friends on a regular basis.

11. Compared to your life ten years ago, would you say you have more or less leisure time?

    (1) Less
    (2) About the same
    (3) A bit more
    (4) A lot more

12. How would you compare the amount of time you spend running errands today with the amount you spent ten years ago?

    (1) More
    (2) About the same
    (3) Somewhat less
    (4) A lot less

13. During the past year, how many books would you estimate you've read from beginning to end?

    (1) 0-2
    (2) 3-5
    (3) 5-10
    (4) 11 or more

14. How good are you at glancing at your watch or a clock without anyone else noticing?

    (1) Very good
    (2) Good
    (3) Fair
    (4) Not good at all

15. How would you rate your ability to conduct a conversation and appear to be paying attention while thinking about something else at the same time?

    (1) Excellent
    (2) Good
    (3) Fair
    (4) Poor

16. How often do you find yourself interrupting the person with whom you're talking?

    (1) Regularly
    (2) Often
    (3) Occasionally
    (4) Rarely

17. When talking on the telephone, are you more likely to:

   (1) Do paperwork, wash dishes, or do some other chore
   (2) Straighten up the surrounding area
   (3) Do small personal tasks (e.g. file nails, reset watch)
   (4) Do nothing else

18. In an average week, how many evening or weekend hours do you spend working overtime or on work you've brought home?

   (1) 16 or more
   (2) 11-15
   (3) 6-10
   (4) 0-5

19. During a typical weekend, do you engage primarily in:

   (1) Work for income
   (2) Household chores and errands
   (3) Leisure activities
   (4) Catching up on sleep and relaxing

20. In a typical year, how many weeks of paid vacation do you take?

   (1) 1 or less
   (2) 2
   (3) 3
   (4) 4 or more

21. On the whole, do you find vacations:

   (1) Frustrating
   (2) Tedious
   (3) Relaxing
   (4) Rejuvenating

22. How often do you find yourself wishing you had more time to spend with family members or friends?

   (1) Constantly
   (2) Often
   (3) Occasionally
   (4) Almost never

23. During a typical day, how often do you feel rushed?

   (1) Constantly
   (2) Often
   (3) Occasionally
   (4) Almost never

24. Which statement best describes your usual daily schedule?

   (1) There aren't enough hours in the day to do everything I have to do
   (2) On the whole I have just about enough time to do everything I have to do
   (3) I can usually do the things I have to do with time left over
   (4) The day seems to have more hours than I'm able to fill

25. During the past year, would you say that your life has grown:

   (1) Busier
   (2) About the same
   (3) Somewhat less busy
   (4) A lot less busy

Scoring:
Add up the total of all numbers circled. A score of 25-40 indicates you are timelocked; 41-55, pressed for time; 56-71 in balance; 72-100 time on hands.

So what have you learnt from this questionnaire[11]? Probably only what you already know, that clock time can prevent you having a good quality of life. I think 'Timelock' has something very useful to say about how time became so hectic, but suffers from the same shortcomings as other time management books. It assumes that the suggestions made are ones we have not come across before. Keyes found in his interviews that, when asked about tactics for managing their time, most respondents listed the contents of a time management program. The point is that we know how to do these things, but they are not working for us. This is the law of diminishing returns at work. The book makes suggestions about what to do to become 'unlocked', but herein lies the problem. The Solutions are things we know how to do, but fail to do, such as taking something off your to-do list before you add something new to it. Or learning to say no, and getting good at it. Yes, I know that if I say no and keep a reasonable number of things to do on my list I will be able to feel more in control. But the point is I don't do it.

This idea is usually addressed by saying that we have not developed our skills enough, but I don't believe this is true. Time is no longer the issue, because there is none, or more precisely, there is none outside of ourselves. For as long as I conceive of time as something that is independent of my body and my senses, I will continue to be a slave to clock addiction and continue to feel timelocked.

The business of busyness

Clock time addiction is my label for the crazy script we act out each day in our conversations, the my-time-is-more scarce-than-yours script I talked about earlier. In the last 5 years the rate at which we feel we have to run to catch up has increased significantly. In the business school where I work, I have to defend the need for our 'short' programmes to stay at 5 days. The demand, which has become louder and louder over the years, is to cut the programmes down to two days because 'busy' executives have no time to think for 5 days.

---

[11] From *Timelock: How life got so hectic and what you can do about it* by Ralph Keyes, 1991. Harper Collins.

We are haunted by the fear that we don't have enough time to do what needs to be done. Do you see yourself in any of the following examples?

- You try to read faster, lead board meetings more efficiently, write reports on the fly, and when you have to talk to your employees you find yourself nodding at a faster and faster rate to encourage them to accelerate.
- You sigh whenever you have to wait. At traffic lights, if there are two lanes and each contains one car, you read the year, make, and model of each car to guess which will pull away most quickly.
- At a supermarket, if you have a choice between two queues, you note the number of people in each and multiply this number by the number of items per trolley. If your calculation is wrong, you feel depressed.
- You find yourself doing or thinking more than one thing at a time. Psychologists call this polyphasic activity, and your working colleagues encourage you to do it. At times, you find yourself standing in the middle of a room wondering what on earth to do as you have lost count of the number of activities you are in the middle of.
- Your car is a favourite place for polyphasic activity. Clock time addicts may drive, eat, drink coffee, listen to tapes for ideas, shave or apply make-up, direct business on the car phone—all at the same time.
- Or they may try to watch TV, read *Leadership*, eat dinner, and carry on a phone conversation simultaneously after getting home from work. This is often defined as relaxation rather than work.

These examples are everyday occurrences in many people's lives and in some ways it is difficult to view this as a problem. If it is the norm, is it abnormal? The answer depends on what you think about the quality of your life as you follow that norm.

The norm looks like this description of the life of a working woman. She knows what to do, and yet she cannot find a way to work and live that is stress free, that gives her all the time in the world whilst making money, and to have today all that she keeps putting off to the future. When she retires she will have time, slow down and enjoy life, and that vision keeps her hooked on the speed of her life today. She knows how to do it differently. She has read all the Time Management books, she has a smartphone, knows stress management techniques, goes to yoga once a week. One day she realises that even the yoga is being used to help the addiction. She drives over an hour to get there, spends all that time on the mobile phone finishing off work calls, and makes plans for that evening after yoga. She goes to bed that night reflecting on how tired she feels, but how lucky she is to know how to take care of her well-being. She has this work-life balance thing under control. After 6 hours sleep her day starts again. She is doing all the 'right' things and yet... life feels just as hectic as ever, just as busy as ever and she is doing so much more today than she was 10 years ago.

Outlined above is a composite of the kind of life many people I talked to for this book actually live. And these are the lucky ones, who at least in behaviour if not in intent, do things to help themselves be well. The majority of people I work with are slaves to clock addiction in both intent and behaviour. Both in and outside of the workplace rushing has become a way of life that has been accepted as the way things have to be and is never challenged. If you need a lengthy example of this kind of life you need go no further than Kate Reddy.[12] She is the fictional hero of all clock addicts today, from a book titled 'I don't know how she does it'. Kate prides herself in living the kind of life that finds her at 2 in the morning 'faking' mince pies for her kid's school. She buys these at the supermarket and then makes them look home-made when she gets back from her high powered job in a financial institution. Kate gets a large bag of fan mail at the publishers from people who make similar life choices. They are unhappy with their choices, and yet their only way out is to justify those choices as 'just the way things are'.

I do not ask how she does it but why she does it. Maybe she does it because of the rush of adrenaline, the rush of multi-tasking, the rush of being under pressure to get things done quickly or the rush of

---

[12] *I Don't Know How She Does It* by Alison Pearson, 2003. Vintage.

being in control at last. The key point here is that all this behaviour is a short-term illusion. We are totally out of control but do not know it. We are addicted. An addiction is formally defined as a self-destructive behaviour that temporarily fills an unmet need.

If you are a clock time addict, then you will recognise this repetitive destructive pattern. You try to change your way of working and living, only to keep finding yourself doing the same thing you say you don't want to do. You suspect that your behaviour is being driven by something other than conscious thought, but dismiss that suspicion each time it comes up. A drunk does not want to drink, he just can't help himself, the addict does not want to inject heroin, she just finds herself stealing from her family to buy the drug, and the smoker can give up anytime he likes; he jokes he has done so hundreds of times before. My contention is that we use clock time like a drug. Fast time is like smoking those cigarettes and slow time is like giving them up. We know how to do it because we have already slowed down hundreds of times before.

Peter Senge[13] calls the process I describe above 'shifting the burden'. It works like this: you think that you solve a problem by applying what he calls a symptomatic solution, in our case managing clock time. This then diverts attention away from more fundamental solutions. However, the symptomatic solution has side effects, in this case a sense that our lives are running out of time. An addiction is established when the sense of being out of time overwhelms our capacity to manage clock time, but we keep looking to that symptomatic solution to 'solve' the problem of lack of time.

A fundamental solution might be to look at the limitations of clock time, but this is harder to see than the more obvious link between getting things done and managing clock time. This means that we find it easier to keep our focus on the addiction and feel that the locus of control is external to us. So you say to all who will listen that you are doing your best, but that somehow you keep finding yourself in the same spot with horrifying regularity. The 'solution' that you apply when you have 'no time', is to review your time management system and move activities around, but asking yourself what else you could

---

[13] In *The Fifth Discipline*. 1990. Century Business.

do to have more time is the quick fix. You try the quick fix more and more, the problem comes and goes so you feel you 'can quit whenever you want' and your ability to perceive the fundamental solution that will make the problem disappear declines. During the few times in the year when you have time to stop you have that gnawing feeling that there is more to this problem than your time management skills. And then you get back on the treadmill.

The question we never ask is: how would I solve the problem of not having enough time if Time Management was not an option? What are my alternatives? The goal of having more time is not being addressed by the quick fix. If it were, we would feel that today we have all the time we want for living our lives, judging by the details of our schedules. But the opposite is true for many of us.

The diseases of clock time

Steven Covey[14], amongst others, talks about urgency addiction and defines its symptoms very clearly. We find ourselves experiencing a predictable and reliable sensation, although it may not be a pleasant sensation. We find that the sense of urgency becomes the primary focus and absorbs our attention during experience. We feel better as the focus on urgency temporarily eliminates emotional and physical pain, and as we feel more in control we feel an artificial sense of self-worth, power, intimacy, accomplishment, intensity, and spontaneity. What happens over time is that our problems worsen and negative emotions increase. When urgency addiction gets really problematic we experience a loss of true relating, often leading to the loss of relationships. The fictional character Kate Reddy comes home one day late from work to find that her husband has left her.

Addiction to urgency is used to mask fundamental unmet human needs. We create the pressure in our lives in order to feel, only in the short-term, certain basic needs have been met – i.e. Peter Senge's symptomatic solution. What are some of these basic needs? The need to feel useful, to earn approval, to protect ourselves from

---

[14] In *First Things First* by S. R. Covey, A.R. Merrill and R.R Merrill,. 1997. Simon & Schuster Publications.

feeling vulnerable, for a life purpose and meaning, to feel secure and the need to follow a work ethic to be accepted by society. Because of demands in our working environment we only go for the quick fix to meet our needs. In the long term, not only have we not solved the problem, but also our ability to see that the quick fix does not solve it is reduced more and more. We then feel more and more out of control and more and more ashamed that even though we are doing it all by the book, the problem remains. We deny that there is a problem in order to rationalise our inability to solve it. We find ourselves in a painful cycle, one which lies at the root of our need to collude with each other on the issue of lack of time, and on the 'fact' that this is just they way things are and will continue to be.

Our expectations of what we can accomplish have become a dysfunctional fantasy, fed by books with titles such as: 'How to accomplish more in half the time', or 'Achieve twice as much in half the time'. These books fuel our fear that we are just not competent enough, and that if we only had one more tip on how to manage time or ourselves more effectively we might be able to squeeze one last activity out of that half hour. Our perceived sense of 'too fast' is created by our insistence on feeding the fantasy that we are, or can become, an unlimited capacity machine. I believe that we are addicted to clock time because it creates the illusion that with enough learning, training, intelligence, emotional or otherwise, we can become that mythical being who has finally cracked the secret of the ever-stretching hour.

Other authors have talked about hurry-sickness, or time urgency to describe our tendency to do as much as possible in as short a period of time as possible. Meyer Friedman and Ray Rosenman looked at the links between heart disease and behaviour. They created what became known as the type A personality. The typical coronary prone personality was impatient, walked quickly, ate quickly, did more than one thing at once and was proud to be always on time. Different scales for measuring this type of behaviour have been developed, for example, the Speed and Impatience scale, the Time Urgency scale and the Perpetual Activation scale.

However, Robert Levine[15], warns us not to over-generalise from these findings. Individuals have a different pace of action in different situations. It is not necessarily true that fast is bad and slow is good, and it seems that our ability to be what he calls 'multitemporal' is more important for our health. His suggestion of what to do if you are worried is to do a personal stock-take of how you are in comparison to others in certain areas of your life. Think about 2 or 3 close work colleagues or friends, take pen and paper and create a table with names at the top and the following subjects at the side:

1. Concern with clock time
2. The speed of your speech pattern and your patience (or lack of it) with those who have slower speech patterns than you
3. Rushed eating
4. Walking speeds
5. Driving – or how frustrated do you get by slow traffic?
6. Extent to which you are driven by your schedule
7. List making activity
8. Nervous energy -how irritable do you become if you have to sit for, say, one hour doing nothing?
9. Waiting – or how frustrated do you become when life makes you stop and wait?
10. Alerts – do other people warn you to slow down?

Answer each question in turn for each person on your table and you should develop a picture of how you are in relation to your peers. This will enable you to decide if you should be worried about your tendency to time urgency or not.

Levine says that nearly everyone will show a tendency to time urgency in at least one of these areas. If your stock-take tells you that you score higher than most people around you in most of these areas, or if you have a particularly high score on one, then if you were to take the actual test you would be likely labelled as a time-urgent personality. If you have extreme scores on the time-urgency

---

[15] *A Geography of Time - the temporal misadventures of a social psychologist* by Robert Levine, 1997. Basic Books. A book about 'how every culture keeps time a little bit differently'.

scales then you are likely to be labelled hurry sick. Diane Ulmer and Harry Schwartzburd coined this term in 1996 when looking at time pathologies. If you are worried, they suggest that you focus on 3 symptoms. Do you notice:

- A deterioration of your personality – particularly marked by lack of interest in anything that is not achievement oriented in your life. A tendency to evaluate life in terms of quantity rather than quality.
- A racing mind – the speed of your thoughts is getting so fast that you can focus your attention less and less on any one thought. A tendency for disrupted sleep.
- Loss of ability to accumulate pleasant memories – your mental focus is on the past or on worries about the future. A tendency to only focus on the present when there is an unexpected crisis that leads to maintaining memories of such unpleasant situations.

If you answer yes to these questions you have a hurry sickness and you are more likely to suffer from cardiovascular problems.

The director of the Meyer Friedman Institute[16], Barton Sparagon, is very clear about the cause for hurry sickness: the prevalence of technology in our working lives – e-mail, mobile phones, pagers and laptops. We can, and do, bring work home, into our bedrooms and on our holidays. He believes that this has led to time speeding up for many of us, and that there is increased pressure to do more in the same number of hours. We feel what he calls a sense of entitlement – a sense that we have a god given right to get our way without delay. We say, why should anyone slow me down? We become less and less respectful of each other. More than just politeness is at stake here, Sparagon suggests. Such chronic impatience damages not only our social environment, but also our physical health. As impatience builds, it doesn't take long before explosion point is reached, and impatience is equally damaging for those who repress it.

The high-tech revolution and our contemporary lifestyles have

---

[16] www.ucsf.edu.

brought with them many serious health problems, including heart attacks, palpitations, depression, anxiety, immune disorders, digestive problems, insomnia and migraines. Sparagon says that human beings are not designed for prolonged, high-speed activity. 'When you look at our heart rates, brain wave patterns – our basic physiology has not evolved to keep pace with the technology. He say that we are hard-wired so we are able to cope with a 'fight-flight' response where: 'the stress ends within five to ten minutes. In our current culture though, we struggle for hours on end.' An organism constantly in a state of fight-flight can only do two things: fight or escape.

Sparagon used to see problems such as weakened immune systems, irritable bowel, migraines, and anxiety disorders primarily in the 40 to 50-year-old age group, but he increasingly treats in his practice 20 and 30-year-olds. Many of the young men and women asking for help with problems like high blood pressure, digestive problems and headaches are full-time employees juggling home and work life. The long-term health consequences of hurry sickness are not mild ones. 'People can't maintain stress disorders without getting more severe problems like inflammatory bowel disease' says Sparagon. Hypertension puts us at greater risk of a heart attack, and a suppressed immune system can lead to increased risk for cancer.

Even children are not spared. He sees an epidemic of symptoms like hypertension, migraines and digestive problems in children as young as 10, disorders never before seen in children. These problems may be the result of being absorbed into the frenetic pace of their parents' lives. Or they may be the result of too many extracurricular activities and unprecedented homework requirements. Children are experiencing the same sense of overload, time pressure and demands that their parents experience, and they don't have the coping mechanisms to deal with it.

Robert Levine is critical of this analysis. He argues that a rapid tempo in and of itself does not always mean disease. External time pressures do not always lead to time urgency nor do either of these always lead to the symptoms of hurry sickness. Individuals have a very different notion of what counts as fast and what counts as slow. We have a preferred inner tempo in relation to different areas of our lives: work, city or town where we live, home life, social life and also our lives as a whole. Time urgency is only one aspect of tempo. Other aspects are to do with the perceived speed of other people at work, speed outside of work, preferred level of activity and preferred tempo in our surrounding environment. In other words, how we relate to time has a lot to do with how we perceive our bodies and the environment around us, what we call lived time.

Robert Levine says that we may be more at risk if our inner tempo does not match the tempo of life around us, rather than simply saying that fast tempos are bad. This is easy to say, but if I asked you to talk to me about your preferred inner tempo, would you know much about it? Knowing the characteristics of our inner sense of time is further complicated by the possibility of entrainment, which is a characteristic of biological systems that applies to us humans. Basically, this means that we are not as independent from those around us as we would like to believe. A flock of geese only becomes a flock because of entrainment. They pick up on each other's inner rhythms and stabilise on a common rhythm that is shared by all. Women who live together pick up on their menstrual rhythms and have periods at the same time each month. Given this information, how can you know without doubt your own inner tempo?

Specialists try to frighten us into slowing down. If we don't do something different with our lives, they warn, we will die way too young. It is as simple as that. But – just as with smoking – we refuse to change paths, stopping is not an option but we can at least be proud of being fast. We advertise the fact that 'mums are now faster than ever' and this is why they now have impregnated polish wipes to rush through housework even faster. We are indeed victims of comfort. This advert shows Mum proudly throwing away the wipe. A wipe that goes to the tip, that goes into our landfills, and that most probably does not bio-degrade for years.

The diseases of clock time are a shared experience for many of us in the United Kingdom and America at least. I will use the clock time addiction in the rest of this book to refer to what we have explored in this chapter. Clock time leads to 'dis-ease'.

Lived time is a different kind of time, it makes time make sense, and brings life back to life. Lived time will be explored in depth in chapters 3 and 4. It is a kind of embodied time that is non-linear and that can do what clock time cannot. Time inside a person's head is different from clock time; it is more flexible, and more malleable. Robert Pollack tells us that our perception of the outside world can be slowed, stopped or reversed by the ticking of a number of internal clocks.[17] Clearly time exists beyond the inside of a person's head, but our perception can alter how we relate to the outside world when time is located within and not without. We often feel confused and stressed because our inner time says one thing, but the clock says something completely different. We keep trying to teach ourselves not to listen to our bodies by applying the 'wisdom' of clock time relentlessly to anything and everything. Not everything that counts can be counted. There is more to life than increasing its speed, and there is more to time than clocks. Such simple idioms reflect a truth forgotten in our efficient clock time world.

It is likely that we have reached the limit of what we can do in the time we have. I feel that the quality of our decision-making and action has already deteriorated beyond an acceptable point. We are going too fast to see the consequences of our actions. We have developed a faulty time sense, and a mistaken appreciation of what it will take to re-connect with a real sense of time.

The background anxiety you and I feel as we wonder how we do it all is a perfectly normal response to a lifestyle that does not sustain life. The anxiety may be telling us to stop because we are going too fast on the road to nowhere. We have no built in warning system to tell us we are just going too fast, in the way that cars in Japan beep when the speed limit is exceeded. Perhaps we need to develop an inner beeper. We do not need drugs to help us with our ability to attend to the world, but we need to pay attention to attention. We need to develop our ability to attend in a stable way. This stable attention can be learnt, and is a pre-requisite to being able to develop any new behaviour. Part of this book will attend to attention, practices to develop a serviceable mind. Did you know that our ability to maintain our attention in a sustained way on an object of our choice without getting distracted is a mere 3 seconds on average? Many people do much worse than that, and we can all do better. Our ability to develop

---

[17] *The Missing Moment*. Robert Pollack, 1999. Houghton Mifflin.

an embodied sense of time is dependent on developing our ability to attend to the world and ourselves.

We keep rushing because we are terrified of being left out, or feeling a loser, or being one of those people at work that just could not cope! There is a choice, but the cost is so high that we feel we have to do whatever it takes to keep accelerating, and not just accelerating but doing it faster than the rest. When we live in the fast lane and we slow down, we get run over. And this is more than a figure of speech in a world that has forgotten that time is not literally money. Being a slave to clock time may well turn out to be the high that brings us down, unless we are willing to re-develop our sense of time to mean more than how good we are at keeping appointments.

A principle too far[18]?

An expert in personal and organisational effectiveness offered sardonically the following notes for 'improvement' on Shubert's unfinished symphony:

- The 12 violins all play the same note; it is an unnecessary duplication of effort. I suggest, therefore, that the number of violins is reduced
- The oboists have nothing to do for a significant amount of time. We should make them redundant and distribute their work equally throughout the whole orchestra
- It is inefficient to have the horns repeat the same passage that has already been interpreted by the piano
- If these redundancies were eliminated 20 minutes of the concert would be saved
- The symphony has 2 movements. Shubert should have achieved his musical objectives in one

In sum – If he had paid attention to this timesaving feedback he would have had time to finish his symphony!

---

[18] Anonymous. I translated this from the Spanish as colleagues in South America sent it to me. I would value knowing more about its providence. Write to me at the publishers.

A FAULTY SENSE OF TIME

Clock time does help us get things done, but it takes time's centre of gravity outside of ourselves and into the clock. When we look at the clock to check if we are hungry, I conclude that we have taken a useful tool too far. Clock time may help us get to meetings on time, but it has also led to us developing faulty sensory perception. We have become unable to perceive, see, hear and feel some of the limitations of living in clock time. Specialists note such disorders as hurry sickness and urgency addiction, but we turn these disorders into the currency with which to measure success. We are not successful unless we suffer from some of these disorders. It is better to be type A than to be type B if we want to attain that directorship.

Time researcher Dale Southerton also notes the negative impact a shift 'from collectively maintained temporal rhythms towards individually defined movements in time and space'[19] has caused in our perception of time. We have greater levels of informality and flexibility, but one negative side effect of this is that 'the potential for co-ordinating practices between social actors is increasingly problematic'.[20] Being individually efficient in clock time makes it hard for us get together. Getting together takes time as we need to co-ordinate schedules, and this adds to our sense of being rushed. We do not stop to question the wisdom of flexibility, because it appears to bring more individual efficiency. Our sloppy perception does not notice the time that now disappears in our desperate attempts to co-ordinate ways to be in the same place at the same time. In this chapter I will show the limitations of clock time. I will help you refine the lens of your perception, and challenge your own assumptions about clock time as the only way to live. You may choose to continue to shelter under the clock, but by the end of this chapter you will understand that we pay a high price to live in clock time.

A faulty sense of time is partly determined by our insistence on using time management to solve problems that are not tractable with a reductionistic model of time. Please complete the questionnaire below, and do not read on until you have answered each question honestly with a yes or a no.

---

[19] In 'Squeezing time' by Dale Southerton, *Time and Society*, Vol. 12, no1 (2003).
[20] Ibid.

2. A faulty sense of time

1. Do you ever rush more than you planned?
2. Has your need to rush and go faster ever interfered with your ability to do your job?
3. Is your need to rush causing conflict with your spouse or other family members?
4. Do you feel depressed, guilty, or remorseful when you are unable to carry out all the activities you had planned in a given time period?
5. Do you use whatever time you have almost continuously until your time is exhausted?
6. Do you have an obsession to get more time when you are asked to do something and cannot find a way to schedule it in?
7. Have you ever experienced chest pains or rapid or irregular heartbeats when in a great hurry?
8. Do you have difficulty sleeping without taking a drink or a drug?
9. Are you absorbed by the thought of your time pressures even when interacting with a friend or loved one?
10. Have you begun to hurry even when you are alone or when relaxing on a weekend?
11. Do you ever have feelings that people are talking about you or watching you?
12. Do you find yourself putting more and more activities into your day?
13. Have you tried to stop and slow down your pace of life and found that you could not?
14. Have any of your friends or family suggested that you might have a problem?
15. Have you ever lied or misled those around you about how much and how often you are focused on your lack of time?
16. Do you find yourself rushing in public places?
17. Are you afraid that if you stop hurrying your work will suffer, you will lose energy, motivation or confidence?
18. Do you spend time with people, or in particular places, only because they help you feel good about your constant hurrying?

19. Have you ever 'stolen' time from your friends and family?
20. Do you feel guilty when you allow yourself to do nothing for a given period?

These questions are not a validated tool to determine how faulty your time perception is. However, the more yes answers you have given the more likely it is that you cannot see that there is any other way to live than under the shadow of clock time. The origin of these questions may well be familiar to some readers, as they are the kind of diagnostic questions used by most Addiction Recovery 12-step programmes. This version was adapted from 'Cocaine Anonymous: A self-test for cocaine addiction'. I took out references to cocaine and replaced them with references to time and hurry. So don't panic; for yes responses to outnumber no responses is perfectly normal. We live in a culture of immediacy, a culture that has tough penalties for making the choice to stop and question the wisdom of the clock.

The price we pay for living in clock time

Because the negative consequences of living in clock time are rarely foregrounded or examined, many of us fail to make the choice to view our relationship to time through a different lens. We look to manage time better, but don't look at the way we are living. We ask time management to give us the quality of life we crave, but never ask if the way we live might itself be part of the problem.

We allow the clock to run our lives and find sophisticated rationalisations for doing this. A root of the problem lies in a little promise we keep making to ourselves: one day the pressures of time will be gone and I will have found the right work-life balance. As mentioned in chapter 1, we get a glimpse of what that balance might be, but only a glimpse, and then we are back on the treadmill. The treadmill always runs at a speed just beyond that which we can comfortably keep. If only I were fitter I would be able to easily keep up and be happy, but the treadmill has a mind of its own and as we get fit enough to keep up, it again increases its speed – just beyond that which we can cope with. The speed keeps increasing until we feel

2. A faulty sense of time

out of control again and press the emergency stop button. Years go by and we keep promising ourselves: one day the balance will be right or at least it will be right for longer.

> '*I wanted everything, and I got what I wanted but there was no existential coherence. I was fragmented inside and out. I was simply unable to integrate the disparate, dangling threads of an over-full life. Individually and singly, the threads could not be joined together into a meaningful whole. Try as I might, I couldn't 'get it together'. Unable to let any one thing go, yet overwhelmed by keeping everything simultaneously under control, I created elaborate coping mechanisms, which I perceived would get me through. Well intentioned and dedicated as I was, I was frantic and frayed, and my life remained disconnected.*
>
> *In retrospect I see I was playing right into that grand deception: it's your life; do with it what you want. I had made my life the centre of the universe, even under the guise of serving others. Despite my efforts to live selflessly, I was trapped in the madness of a middle-class lifestyle that revolved – not only ultimately, but in the most mundane ways – around my wants and desires. I just couldn't see that this kind of living was unreal, untrue. No matter how many ways I tried to compensate for the lack of synthesis in my life, it wasn't until I stopped living on terms centred on personal fulfilment and independence that I began to find some sense of coherence. And I saw that I had a choice to make: I could continue living in that way, negotiating a multiplicity of demands and relationships of my own choosing; or I could begin anew on an altogether different foundation, one where community (not self) and mutual service (not personal fulfilment) were the premise.*'
>
> Charles Moore[21]

It is possible to hold all these threads together. It is possible to hold a complex network of relationships that allow us to have it all: the best yoga teacher, the best exhibitions, the best spouse, the best scenery

---

[21] In *Drained: Stories of people who wanted more* by Johan Christoph Arnold, 1999. The Plough Publishing House.

for each time of the year. So what is the problem? The problem is a feeling that is named and made true by this story, that feeling of deep exhaustion at holding the dream together, the sense that life lacks any element of surprise and the surprises that do come are unwelcome. I see the truth of this story in my own life. I can set goals and achieve them, I can want things and get them, I can choose my work, and the people I work with. However, deep down if I stop long enough to listen, there is a provisional quality to my life. A sense that having it all is not enough, but I keep trying to integrate the disparate and dangling threads anyway because to do anything else would be to admit failure.

I visited New Zealand a few years ago. One day I was sitting by a beautiful waterfall, talking to a friend who had decided to 'fail'. She left a successful career in Britain and moved to a simple house by the sea, where she had a child and a husband but no money. As we talked about our life choices, I told her that she had taken the easy way out and that I would continue to look for a way in which I could have my career and also the right quality of life. When we live in clock time we do not have certain choices open to us. Genuine options are labelled failure and nobody wants to be a failure. My friend had courage and, I now see, she certainly had not taken the easy way out. She understood that making a choice was just that. If you chose path A, you did not walk down path B. It is that simple. We tell ourselves that one day we will choose a new lifestyle too. But is it really that simple? Few of us make new choices, even when we can afford to[22]. It is easier to keep pretending that one day I will not have to choose, and that one day I will have it all.

The ethos of training and development in the workplace carries the same kind of unspoken assumption, that if people are developed enough then they can have it all and the organisation can also have it all. If life does not quite fit with this assumption just yet, it is because

---

[22] Read *The Working Life: The promise and betrayal of modern work* by Joanne Ciulla, 2000. Three Rivers Press. She explores interesting data. One great story is that of the millionaire who gives his wife millions in stock as a birthday present, and finds her next morning cutting out discount coupons from the newspaper. Her general point is that few people change their lifestyles even when they have achieved financial independence and the book then goes on to explore the more fundamental purposes of work.

people have not been on enough development activities, or have not yet been with the right person to teach them what they need to learn. The responsibility is firmly put on the individual to learn the right skills, and those who do not buy into the need to develop and be life-long learners are said to be inflexible. Flexibility is all in the workplace of today, and once labels have been given to people, their career options can become severely limited. So, do we really have a choice? What kind of a choice is it, when the consequences are such that we are forced to go down one path only?

Joanne Ciulla in her book *The Working Life* talks about the power dynamics implicit in what she labels the therapeutic approach to work. She argues that most training and development is aimed at 'adapting people to society, not engaging them in a public dialogue about what society should be.' She feels this approach encourages either an enthusiastic or a sceptical adaptation to work, instead of 'public participation in shaping the goals and values of the workplace'.

She further argues that it is impossible to assess the value of initiatives when employees are living a work ethic of fear. In the current economic situation organisations have little control over the global economy. Redundancies are, therefore, not about personal responsibility but the fault of unseen global forces in the economy. Ciulla believes that uncertainty based fear of the future forces many of us to work at a frantic pace. If you add to this the fact that an employee's number one fear is to comment on their bosses' management style, the undiscussables of the workplace[23], you could conclude that any improvement in performance from development initiatives, such as coaching or team-working skills, might be the result of fear. This is fear of survival within an unfair system, if you look at real work beyond training courses. Ciulla concludes that whilst the incomes of the rich have gone up in the past 30 years, middle-income earners have only just kept pace with inflation and for low-income workers, their real wages actually fell. A quick glance at the wage differential between both successful and failing executives and the so-called average worker, and the work and income scenario seems remarkably unfair.

---

[23] Ibid, p146.

Can we genuinely say that there is a choice not to work at a frantic pace? We know that we can lose our job at a moment's notice. We know that fundamentally most organisations are run with a 'get-it-while-you-can' attitude with little attention paid to the long-term. We know that the economy could fall apart any moment, and that more and more of what we find meaningful in life is located in work and not outside of it. This work ethic of fear is a real driver to keep us living in clock time. Constant fear is a price we pay for clock time. We do not want to have the consequences of certain choices, and that keeps us choosing unsustainable lifestyles. Our choices are not always taken consciously; they reflect fundamental beliefs that often unconsciously drive our behaviour.

An illustration of this point is found in this summary of a thought experiment devised by Ciulla.[24] Harry and Mary are 2 employees of ACME Inc. They do the same job and receive the same benefits. When it came to performance review time they both got the same scores. Both work to very high standards. Harry is not married and does not have many out of work interests, so he often works 10 to 14 hour days. Mary is married, with 3 children and is active in her church and community. She works a normal 8-hour day. The company keeps telling both of them that it is the quality of their work that is most important. But they do not believe the company. The question: If management had to choose to make one of them redundant which one would they choose? Take time to think about this. It really highlights the often unspoken issues that keep us working at a frantic pace even when we have a choice to do otherwise.

If we believe that in choosing a different way we will be labelled less successful and possibly lose our jobs, then it is not surprising that we keep going through the same cycles and do not change our behaviour. We would not choose to be 'less-than' in a marketplace that makes decisions based on quantity and not necessarily quality. So we do not explore the 'less-than' path. It is as if it did not exist. For we would not want to do something that gives less recognition, less money, less spending power, less shopping time. That is no choice at all.

---

[24] Ibid, p160.

2. A faulty sense of time   53

Another price we pay for clock time is an inability to perceive certain choices as valid. Choice becomes defined, by implication, as an activity, which if done well can give you a life without consequences. Work-life balance often means that the scales are never in a state of equilibrium for very long. This is accepted as the 'way things are these days', rather than challenged as 'not the way they should be'.

The search for work-life balance in the world of work[25] has led to many initiatives, but little decrease in hours worked is evident in today's workplace. In fact we are working longer hours. Work has become home for less pay. The popularity of these initiatives is a sign of the desperation that working people feel about the quality of their lives, not necessarily a sign that any fundamental solution is forthcoming. As an approach it does little more than reify our slavery to clock time. The only choice, reads the subtext, is to find a balance within the parameters defined by a get-it-while-you-can attitude to business.

Even the notion of balance is precarious as anything can throw the balance off. The responsibility for keeping the balance is the individual's, who has to develop the skill to get that balance. The organisation will offer flexible working and other perks, but cannot force us to take them. Hochschild[26] tells us that the reality of work today is that employees do not choose to take what the company offers to help with work-life balance. Ciulla argues that it is the work ethic of fear that is at play here, she suggests that Hochschild's employees may have sensed that there was a conflict between benefits offered and job security. Hochschild herself quotes a line from the employee handbook 'Time spent on the job is an indication of commitment. Work more hours'. It is clear that Mary and not Harry would suffer if they worked in the company researched by Hochschild.

A choice exists between one temporal lifestyle and another, but there is an element of covert coercion, based on a work ethic of fear, that is often at play in our working lives. From this, we can argue that work-life balance initiatives will never fully succeed unless the

---

[25] See, for example, 'The guide to work-life balance' in *People Management*, September, 2002.
[26] In the *Time Bind: When work becomes home and home becomes work* by A. Russell Hochschild, 1997. Henry Holt and Co.

underlying fear is tackled. A cynic might say that this is precisely why companies are investing in these initiatives. Employers offer choices to employees, and say they are at a loss to understand the reason for the lack of take up of what is on offer. Individual workers have responsibility. We are often under the 'illusion of indispensability'[27] and have to let go of this illusion to have genuine choice. The responsibility is, however, shared. Organisations that want change must look at their practices and policies in relation to long-term employment, as well as the short-term fix of a work-life balance programme.

The main point here is that we are not choosing to be clock time addicts. The metaphor of the balancing act between work and life gives us the impression that it is possible to keep both sides of the scales just so. However, it is not so.

We may need to run training programmes on the death of choice – in the sense of being able to have it all. To rebuild our sense of time we have to develop skills for reconnecting with necessity or 'correctness'. In the sense intended by Jean Liedloff in *The Continuum Concept*[28], 'correct' in this context is a tricky word. It does not imply that we all agree on what we want the results of our actions to be, as our intellectual ideas of what we want vary from person to person. What is meant here by 'correct' is that which is appropriate to the ancient continuum of our species inasmuch as it is suited to the tendencies and expectations with which we evolved. 'Expectation in this sense is founded as deeply in man as his very design. His lungs not only have, but can be said to be, an expectation of air...' Leidloff continues this analogy by saying that his eyes not only have, but can be said to be, an expectation of light rays, and his ears have: 'an expectation of vibrations caused by the events most likely to concern him, including voices of other people; and his own voice an expectation of ears functioning similarly in them'.

---

[27] J. Ciulla. Op cit. Page 190. She quotes Lawrence Shames who tells us that we work 16 hour days because we don't want to share work, that we are 'greedy for the illusion of indispensability'.

[28] In *The Continuum Concept* by Jean Liedloff, 1985. Addison-Wesley, paperback, 20th printing. Page 35.

2. A faulty sense of time

We have sacrificed correct action and awareness of expectations for the benefits of clock time. We have lost connection with what it means to be a human being with the 'expectations' of a human being. We have, in short, lost our senses. We think we are free to choose, but we have become unable to notice how little we actually do choose.

When we come back to our senses, through a discipline that commits us to learn to notice the consequences of our actions to our mind and our body, we learn that we don't even have the choice to stand up from a sitting position without tensing our muscles. We learn that we can only learn to have 'free wont', as philosophers sometimes tell us. The Alexander Technique has been such a discipline for me through the last 13 years. When I started I just wanted to learn the technique quickly, fix my backache, and get on with my life. There was no place for backache in my life, and there certainly was not a place for anybody to tell me that perhaps I should look at the way I was living for the cause of my pain. For an hour in those early lessons, I was forced to stop and attend. I was forced to notice that I had no choice over the endless race going on in my head, and no choice to get up from a chair without unnecessarily tensing muscles. The Alexander Technique teaches of the dangers of 'end-gaining' and of neglecting the 'means-whereby' we achieve our ends. A price we pay for clock time is a life focused only on end-gaining, on efficiency and tangible quick results.

> *'Clever mental techniques miss the point if they leave in place the same questing, restless attitude of mind. Instead of calling a meeting to 'discuss' the problem, you call one to 'brainstorm' it, or to get people to draw it with crayons. But the pressure for results, the underlying impatience is still there.'*
> Guy Claxton[29]

---

[29] In *Hare Brain and Tortoise Mind: Why intelligence increases when you think less*, 1997. Fourth Estate.

It has taken me 13 years to accept that I actually do not have total freedom of choice. My intellect tells me I have choice, but my body knows otherwise, and we need to reconnect with our body to correct our faulty time sense. Authentic choice means selecting from alternatives, it does not mean stretching time so that we can do it all and not choose. We say no to what we don't want to do, and think we are choosing. It is easy to reject what we don't want. It is harder to select from all that we do want to do.

We take pride in being a generation of choosers. Guy Claxton believes contemporary young people – as well as many of their parents – belong to a generation of choosers. 'As traditional sources of indigenous authority lose their power, and diverse cultures intermingle, so more and more people are confronted not with a narrow range of life options and adaptations but a vast array of choice. Shall we have a child? Shall we live in Kidderminster, Kansas or Khartoum? Shall we have your mother to live with us or put her in a home? What does it mean to be 'good'? How can I construct a satisfying life, a stable identity, out of the existential supermarket in which I find myself? The pressure to be a learner not just on the surface, but deep down in the moral code of one's life, is intense.'[30] And yet we are paralysed by choice. We really don't know how to choose well. We fail to see the logical impossibility of having both A and Not-A. I keep working at a frantic pace because I want all that money can buy. I keep blaming the clock because it is easier than coming face to face with my fear of uncertainty, and easier than accepting that I have less control of life events than the clock tells me I have.

The price we pay for clock time living is self-deception[31] – an inability to see that we have a problem that is both affecting our life and impacting on others. Terry Warner in a book called *Bonds That Make Us Free* tells us that there is one choice we are always free to make: we can choose to do the right thing by other people or not. Furthermore, we have a deep sense of what that right thing is. When

---

[30] In *Wise up* by Guy Claxton, 1999. Bloomsbury. Page 18.
[31] What follows is based on the work of Terry Warner. His book *Bonds That Make Us Free*, Shadow Mountain Press, 2001. The Arbinger Institute uses these ideas in their work with organisations. www.arbinger.com.

2. A faulty sense of time 57

we are not true to that sense, we betray ourselves, and self-betrayal is at the root of clock time living,

- We get in the lift and see somebody coming. We have a feeling we should wait for him and yet find ourselves pressing the close door button repeatedly
- We see somebody sitting opposite us on the train and feel like we would like to smile at her. We find ourselves looking out of the window instead.
- We want to pick up the phone to talk to that friend who has just experienced a bereavement, and yet decide to ignore that feeling and continue working through our to-do list at work.
- We want to say hello to other drivers, when we are stuck in a traffic jam, instead we find ourselves determinedly looking straight ahead or changing the CD.

The book *Bonds That Make Us Free* explores complex examples of this deep sense of doing right by others. This is something that our society, in the name of efficiency, is making us increasingly used to ignoring. Work offers us plenty of examples: I rush in, notice somebody who looks unhappy, choose to ignore that person and run by them to get to my meeting on time. I come in to give my secretary some work to do, ignore my sense that it would be right to ask how she is and launch into what I want her to do for me. I run into reception to get some papers, notice the receptionist and walk right past her without acknowledging her to grab the papers I need.

Our sense of being human, says Warner, is 'intimately bound up with our capacity to sense something of others' needs and feelings. That is why I call the violation of that sense self-betrayal'. What matters is that when we ignore others we betray our own sense of humanity. This is the start of self-deception. As soon as we betray ourselves, we must find a way of justifying our action. We do that by making the other person wrong in some way. If they are wrong, that allows us to be right. We can visualise ourselves getting caught in the snares of making ourselves right. Warner quotes Pascal: 'it is no doubt an evil to be full of faults, but it is an even greater evil to be full of them and unwilling to recognise them.' Pascal points out that this is because this unwillingness entails the further evil of self-delusion. We are living in a box of self-deception when we are, says Warner: 'convinced that other people and our circumstances are responsible for our feelings and our helplessness to overcome them'. The problem lies not in others but in the self-justifying stories we tell. So, I tell myself that I am busier than the man I see running towards the lift, and that after all I am a senior executive who has important work to do. Or that I have seen that man before and he spends most of his time chatting at the coffee machine!

We can choose to live for others or we can live for ourselves. The I-It mode of life sees others as objects that serve my purpose. The I-Thou mode of life sees others as people in their own right.[32] Self-deception leads us into the I-It mode of life. Warner suggests that we ask ourselves: Do I love myself doing it, or do I love what I am doing? – to find out if we are in the grip of the I-It mode of life. When we love what we do we are receptive to others and out of the box, when we love ourselves doing that thing we are in the box of self-deception and have a lot invested in preserving our 'rightness' in treating others as objects.

> **'People have begun to think of themselves as objects able to fit into the inflexible calculations of disembodied machines: Machines for which the human form-of-life must be analysed into meaningless facts, rather than a field of concern organised by sensory-motor skills. Our risk is not the advent of superintelligent computers, but of subintelligent human beings.'**
> Hubert Dreyfus[33]

When we see others in terms of our own agenda, Warner says, we only see them in relation to our quest to get what we want and people become one of 3 things:

---

[32] A distinction first made in the work of Buber, and quoted in *Bonds That Make Us Free*, 2001.
[33] In *What Computers Can't Do* by H. L Dreyfus, 1979. Harper and Row Publishers.

- An obstacle between me and my goal
- A vehicle to help me get my goal
- An irrelevancy to my goal

In seeing people this way, Warner suggests: 'we become bullies, manipulators, sycophants or snobs'. When we are being driven by clock time we are often in the I-It mode of being. We are the centre of our world and people are the means whereby we achieve our goals. Most of our business affairs are conducted in this mode. We consider those who work in the I-Thou mode as inefficient and 'soft'.

To say that there is no choice to be made, that we can have it all, that it is possible to have a directorship and bring up a child in accordance to the principles of the continuum concept – as expressed in the notion of correctness and expectation mentioned earlier – is to lie to ourselves. We are not just telling ourselves the lie, others are colluding with us in creating the self-justifying stories that make-believe we are not 'really' in control of our time, and that it is the environment that forces us to keep adding more and more to our day. No.

Let me spell it out. The only thing that forces us to continue being clock time addicts is our greed and our unwillingness to consider that it is just possible that we are lying to ourselves. Self-deception is the inability to see that I am the problem. We enter into transactions with others where, says Warner, we agree to be false together. I blame you for giving me too much to do, you blame me for not being efficient enough to get it all done. In blaming you, I get to inflate my own sense of being so important that I get asked to do more than I can do. In blaming me, you get to justify your own sense that nobody is as efficient as you are.

We keep seeing time as the problem and THAT is the real problem. We say: 'it is not my fault, it's just that there is not enough time to get things done', and this does not seem strange to ears used to thinking of time as a limited resource. We even go beyond seeing time as a resource to seeing time as a reified entity that has control over us – we are slaves to the clock and the clock is our master. We say: 'I don't know where my time has gone, I work harder and harder and keep finding myself further and further behind'. Time cannot answer back, and we can blame it for anything that happens in our life. We have a myriad of self- justifying images to prove we are not insane when we argue that one day we will find the magic formula. This is the formula that will allow us to have all the time in the world, and not lose any of the perks of clock time addiction. If I see time as a person who I can blame, I can feel justified when I find myself at the start of yet another year, deciding to get my life under control. It is not my fault, it is time's fault.

We can become aware that personalising time is only a figure of speech, and that time is not really a person. Time is only a convenient invention of man originally created to get groups of people into the same train. Time, in clock time sense, did not exist before this. If we look at clock time as a human invention and stop seeing it as something, or someone that exists out there, then we can more easily see that we use clock time as a drug to keep us from seeing how we deceive ourselves.

We have all found ourselves behaving in ways that are less than respectful to others, and then using a combination of self-justifying excuses for behaving the way we do. If I stop blaming and start looking I might see that my frustrations with time might have to do with my unwillingness to look at myself as somebody who is threatened by my own inability to get everything done that I want to get done. If I stop blaming, I might start questioning the wisdom of what it is that I say I want.

We betray ourselves when we ignore our impulse to do something for somebody, and when we do that we need to tell ourselves a story to make that okay. How does this idea operate in relation to time? We are not saying that we are not treating time right, or that we are somehow disrespectful of time. The self-betrayal here is in relation to other people around me. An example is when I say to myself: 'I should take time to listen'. Sometimes I stop and listen, other times I think of myself as somebody who is so busy and put upon that I 'haven't got the time to stop'. This is where my choice lies. I can choose to acknowledge that I have not taken the time, or I can start to justify my actions to make myself look good in my own eyes and the eyes of others. Clock time living often forces us into justification. I choose I-It mode, get in my box and stop noticing what I am doing. I blame the other person for interfering with my need to achieve my goals, and I view that person as an obstacle.

If I choose I-Thou mode, I still have a choice. I can stop and listen, or I can decide not to listen but without the need to tell others or myself any self-justifying stories about why I behaved the way I did. I can be compassionate towards my shortcomings. Without the need to self-justify I can see myself as an imperfect human that makes mistakes, just like everybody else. The Dalai Lama says that he can get on with everyone because he looks for the common humanity in everyone he meets.[34] Warner tells us that we have the choice to live truthfully: 'We live truthfully when we let the truth about others, including their needs, hopes and fears, guide the way we treat them.' He suggests that it is only by being considerate of others that we live truthfully towards them, and that we need to allow ourselves to be influenced by each person's truth.

We can only treat others in this way if we can find a way to have all the time in the world. We can only have all the time in the world if we are truthful, and stop using time as a justification for our own imperfections. When we live in clock time and see it as the only choice, we forsake our choice to live truthfully. We have to, if we want to keep alive the grand illusion that with enough development we will find the way to become a synthesis between Mother Teresa and Bill Gates.

We do not want to face the fact that we are the kind of person who is afraid, who has limits, who is attached to success for the status it brings, who always wants more out of greed not need, who finally has to admit that there just aren't enough hours in the day to keep loving myself doing what I do, to keep kneeling at the altar of self. It is easier to pay the price of living untruthfully in clock time. Nobody finds it easy to admit that that she or he is scared. We invest a great deal of mental energy pretending that we are fearless and in control. Clock time helps us do that.

The fear of being a zero[35] in society is, alone, enough to keep us choosing clock time, but we often will not admit to being afraid. This

---

[34] In *The Art of Happiness* by Dalai Lama and H. Cutler, 1998. Riverhead Books.
[35] In *The Corrosion of Character* by Richard Sennet, 1998. W. W. Norton and Co.

self-deception keeps us taking actions that may be detrimental to our wellbeing. We measure our worth by how little time we have. We have adopted a value-laden way to talk about cultures that still live in lived time. We disparage them and call them primitive. Then we intervene and make them slaves to the clock in the name of progress. We have learnt to attach positive value to being stressed by work and life to the point that those who are not driven by the clock are labelled the Type Bs of our society. They are not the winners.

If your life is out of balance, you count. You are not a Zero, like the woman at my conference who was laughed at for saying that her life was in balance. We have a lot invested in our attempts at balance not giving us the results we say we want. From the perspective of business success, we know that we will count for less once we have our lives in balance.

Clock time living and more-thinking

> '*Since the advent of the industrial age we have had a terrific word: MORE. It really worked for everything. When our roads became crowded, we built more roads. When our cities became unsafe, we hired more police officers, ordered more police cars, and built more prisons.*'
> Robert Wurman[36]

Clock time encourages us to think of ourselves as unlimited capacity machines. Employee development initiatives perpetuate this belief. I believe that development has a purpose and can genuinely help people manage their jobs better. However, neither technology nor training will allow us to continue to increase capacity in an unlimited way. It is only because we have learnt to live with a faulty sense of time that we believe it is possible to become an unlimited capacity machine. We are reaching a point where 'more-thinking' does not work, and clock

---

[36] In *Information Anxiety* by Wurman, R. S.,1989. Pan Books.

2. A faulty sense of time

time is of a 'morish' nature. Contemporary conventional wisdom tells us that if we keep breaking time up into smaller and smaller units and breaking human activity up into smaller and smaller units then we can have more people doing more in the same amount of time. We act as if this breaking up could go on ad infinitum. We encounter daily the limitations of this policy as it impacts on our quality of life, such as the way we are kept on hold when we call large corporations and the way that people we deal with are not accountable for any meaningful unit of activity. We live with the frustration of having to talk to 5 people to carry out a transaction at a bank, which in the past would have required a 5-minute chat with a friendly bank manager. We are starved of high quality attention in our dealings with others as we live in I-It mode most of our days. Computer manufacturers keep Americans on hold for 3 billion minutes a year.[37] Maybe these are signs that clock time has had a run for its money.

To do time any other way would cost people and organisations money, certainly in the short term and probably in the long term. This is the issue that the quest for the unlimited capacity machine is helping us avoid. The fundamental issue is our greed for profit, and the mantra of efficiency – always get more for less. For as long as we can pretend to be an unlimited capacity machine, or pretend that we are on the way to becoming one, we can keep doing clock time. We can keep getting more for less. More profit for less quality. There is a way to do this right. I just need more development and I will get it. We are encouraged to live exponentially.

'In a pond with water lilies, the number of water lilies doubles each year, Originally there are only a few patches, maybe one-thirty-second of the pond's surface is covered by water lilies. Everyone thinks the pond is lovely, including those who swim in it. The same holds true for the following year, when the water lilies cover one-sixteenth of the surface. But then things start to speed up. The next year one-eighth of the pond is covered with water lilies, a year later one-fourth and the year after that half the pond. Starting with the year that half

---

[37] In *Faster* by James Gleick, 1999. Little, Brown and Company.

the surface is covered with water lilies, there is a maximum of one year left before the entire surface will consist of water lilies.'
Bodil Jonsson[38]

We must accept that there are limits to growth, and that the unlimited capacity machine does not exist in humans any more than it exists anywhere else in nature.

We are already suffering from another negative consequence of 'more-thinking'; we call it consumer choice. A newspaper headline reads[39]: *'Spoiled for choice – 40,000 products in stores, 180 TV channels throw consumers into confusion.'* This reported survey found consumers in Britain are 'being driven to distraction by too much consumer choice'. Some areas of life where the consumer is feeling overwhelmed are: TV channels, supermarket products, mobile phone tariffs, what to have for dinner, breakfast cereals, types of coffee (one chain offers 11 types of coffee, 4 added toppings, 3 different milks, 3 sizes of cup, and the options of decaffeinated and extra cream), books (the average bookshop has 200,000 titles). Tim Harrison of the Abbey National says: 'This is the paradox of progress. More choice, more things to do, more challenges, more decisions, result in more complicated lives'.

In the same article, Michael Wilmott of the Future Foundation says: 'As consumer choice grows, consumers are feeling overwhelmed and it is starting to have a negative impact on their lives'. People are slowly developing coping strategies to minimise choice such as only shopping organic, shopping only on Fridays or buying only trusted brands. But the article does not challenge the assumption that if x is good then 2x must be better. If consumers feel unable to cope, then they have to develop a new shopping strategy. However, it is possible to question the wisdom of an approach to product development that embodies this more-is-best attitude.

I chose not to upgrade my Internet provider's software. As a result, I am at least 3 numbers behind everybody else, because I am

---

[38] In *Unwinding the Clock* by Bodil Jonson, 1999. Harcourt, Inc.
[39] *Daily Mail*, Monday, April 24, 2000.

on version 4 and they are on version 7. The version I have works for my purposes. So why change? I change because everyone else is changing, and I find myself no longer able to receive certain kinds of emails because I have the wrong version of the software. I hear that the newest version of Windows does not even pay lip service to being downward compatible. In the past, good software had to be, but today we are forced to upgrade faster and faster. We have so many new features, so much to learn, and then it is time to change again.

What is it that stops us from challenging 'more-thinking'? It is the fear of being a zero. You mean your computer is 3 years old? Oh, an old machine, I was told when I phoned customer support for help with mine. The subtext was that I was somehow less-than because I had a 3-year-old machine. I then see a picture in a magazine, a mountain of computers with the caption 'businesses have improved very little in their ability to recycle in the last year. As we upgrade our systems more and more often, the waste increases more and more.'[40] This reminds me of my favourite definition of consumerism: so much to live with, and so little to live for. If we chose lived time, we would have to give up the myth of 'more-thinking', but not all of us are prepared to stop being victims of comfort.

Defining success in clock time

Success in clock time is defined as having the temporal lifestyle we want, also the job we want, and also the perfect family, and – if we define our goals well – we might even be able to do some perfect volunteering too. Even if we become successful in these terms, this is not sustainable in the long term. This is why we keep failing at keeping that work-life balance right. Our common sense would tell us this is not sustainable, if only we stopped to listen to it for long enough. We cannot have A and Not-A. It is that simple. We can have peace of mind and all the time in the world, but we have to give up success as defined in clock time.

We also have to give up success as defined by the norms of those around us – bigger and faster cars, bigger and bigger homes, and more

---

[40] Source: The New Economics Foundation, 2001.

and more senior jobs. This is the unpalatable message that most time-management books keep hidden from us. They say we can have all of these things and peace of mind and all the time in the world. I say this is plainly not true. Microsoft and many other organisations pride themselves on hiring only type-A people. So it seems if you want all the time in the world you cannot work for Microsoft.

Many organisations nowadays value efficiency over human values. This means, for example, that employees are required to drive more and more miles to do their job. I have just finished a call with an Operations Director of a fashion logistics firm in which he tells me that he used to be a 1000 miles per week man and now he takes it easy, he only does 500 miles per week. So, you cannot be the Operations Director for this firm if you are not willing to spend that amount of time in the car. When I worked full-time as an Assistant Director for a business school I spent over 120 of my 220 days work per year travelling the world for my work. I could not do my job without doing this. So, if you did not want to live out of a suitcase, you could not have had my job either.

I could go on. There are many trade-offs to be made if you want to have all the time in the world. In striving for success in clock time we keep feeding ourselves the lie that we can define success as having it all, and that our background sense of discontent is only temporary, or is due to lack of skill. We don't want to give up the illusion that we can have goals that lead us to consume more and more and also have all the time we want. This kind of goal is more likely to give you a dose of temporal exhaustion than quality of life. More consumption is a goal that can never be achieved, there will always be more to consume. And more time will always be in the future tense if we refuse to accept the need for trade-offs. Joanne Ciulla says: 'with so many desires and so many choices, some can't or don't choose how they want to live.' In place of personal choice people allow advertisers, employers, or other people's opinions to choose for them. However, if we are prepared to horse trade between a stimulating, highly regarded career, buying stuff, leisure, and security, it is possible to gain power and perhaps improve the quality of our lives. Perhaps controlling our desire to consume is the most difficult trade off, but it can be ultimately liberating. Ciulla concludes: 'The seductive array of

2. A faulty sense of time 67

things that we can buy ties us to our jobs and often deprives us of our time.'[41] This seductive array of things that make up success in clock time, and the promise that there is no need for trade-offs is what keeps us living unsustainable lifestyles.

I started this book talking about how we keep telling ourselves 'I just don't want to live like this anymore' and find ourselves 'living like this' time and time again. I suggested that the cause of this had less to do with the pressures of the modern workplace, and more to do with the way we related to time. I made a distinction between clock time and lived time, and suggested that we are addicted to clock time. We looked at how clock time addiction is detracting from the quality of our lives, and yet we keep looking to the clock to help us re-gain a sense of balance in our lives.

We get some kind of payoff from keeping things as they are. We want to keep playing the game of now-I-have-balance-now-I-don't. It serves a purpose. Keeping lived time as something I get to do on holidays, or will get to do sometime in the future, allows us to do something today. I have suggested that clock time living allows us to keep believing it is possible to have it all; that it is possible to make no trade-offs. This feeds our sense of being in control of our lives when all around us is uncertain and out of control. From this perspective the addictive cycle works. We keep finding ourselves in the familiar place of 'this is just a particularly busy period, it will be better next month', or 'I have made a promise that I will spend more time with the family, I can't break it again'.

We feel a background sense of discontent, blame it on our lack of time, and start juggling work and life again to feel that we are in control of our lives after all. Clock time living helps us feel important and maintain an illusion of indispensability and of being in control. All we need to do, we tell ourselves, is learn to manage our time better. It is possible to do more with less. When we don't question this assumption, we keep putting off a healthy way of life until our report is done, or those figures are complete. However, we justify our behaviour by telling ourselves it is the pressure of the modern workplace that makes us keep doing this. We are temporally

---

[41] J. Ciulla. Op cit. Page 234.

exhausted[42], mentally out of breadth from dealing with immediate demands. We have no energy left for finding a way out of this ever-repeating cycle. Clock time leads to faulty perception. We have developed a faulty sense of time, and one way we can tell is by noticing that background feeling of discontent.

It is hard to accept that it is we who are the problem. It is easier to remain temporally exhausted and not look at the ways in which we contribute to our situation. If I were to look in the mirror for long enough, I would see how my way of life and my choices are the reason for my lack of work-life balance. We don't choose lived time because the price we have to pay is just too high when viewed from the criteria that measure success in clock time. We choose to live in clock time because we make a particular choice with regard to consumption, comfort, money, and status. We like to shop, we like to show off our global travel, we like to drive our big cars. It is this and not time that keeps us feeling like the proverbial hamster.

The signs of a faulty sense of time

Life is not in our bodies

In order to live life in clock time we disconnect from the reality of our own experience. We do not notice that we are tired. We do not notice that we have not stopped to go to the toilet all day. We *wake up* to the fact that the headache we are experiencing may have something to do with not having eaten all day, after a day chasing deadlines. The clock determines everything, if we have no time to eat, then we don't eat. We recognise this sign most obviously when we find this state of affairs to be normal, and tell ourselves that the pace will slow down next week, or next month, but we keep finding ourselves thinking this from month to month. We become more and more detached from life in our bodies, and pour more of ourselves into our checklist existence.

---

[42] The sociologist Elise Boulding coined this term as a way of diagnosing the disease of modern life. Her solution is that we should expand our idea of the present to 200 hundred years into the past and 200 hundred years into the future.

From one of my interviews:

'If I think about today. There is today as a unit of time and then I consciously book the various things. These things that need to be done, turn into tasks that have to get done in a certain amount of time. At its most extreme, it reduces life to a kind of checklist. There is a certain satisfaction in getting those done and thinking, yes, I have achieved something. There is also a sense in которой all that you have done is a checklist.'

We are temporally exhausted

When we are temporally exhausted we tie ourselves in knots. I described this earlier as being mentally out of breadth. We experience terror at the thought that others will find us out, that they may find out that we can't keep up. We feel a need to know everything, even what we don't know, because we are running with no spare capacity. Any unexpected event, no matter how small, is enough to throw us into utter confusion. We just can't afford to get a cold, or for the car to break down, or for the battery of our phone to run out.

When we have to stop, we stop for the minimum amount of time possible. Joanne Ciulla says that for many of us, life is just feeling exhausted from work and then rejuvenating for work. As soon as we recover, and start to connect with our body and ourselves, we are faced with the unresolved issues in our lives. So, we take only enough time out to allow us to get back on the treadmill. Somehow the past disappears, we don't remember the promises we made to take enough time to recharge. The future looms ever more scary. If I don't get up and start again I will be overwhelmed by the amount of work I will have waiting for me on my return. It becomes too much to bear to stay in the silence of our own time rather than the clock's.

We work so hard to have so much in order not to feel pain. The age of self-help manuals has, after all, taught us well how to hanker after that perfect physical, mental and spiritual self. If this perfection is possible and not questioned, then there must be something that I don't know, given that I do not feel like my life is perfect today. I had better get on that treadmill again as I am starting to feel tired and empty. We can create the illusion that we can control nature at the expense of feeling temporally exhausted, as we make that trade everyday.

The test – There are 168 hours in a week[43]
We feel temporally exhausted because we are unable to perceive a simple truth. There are only 168 hours in the week. In reality when we say we want more time, what we mean is we want to do more. We base the number of hours in the week on the understanding that days consist of twenty-four hours, weeks of 7 days, and years of *fifty-two* weeks. Here is what Carole Orsborn suggests we do. Get some paper and: 'do the following calculation. Start with 168 hours. From this, subtract the amount of time you would like to sleep each night times seven. Don't cheat by saying, as you often do, "I can get by on five hours if I have to". This number should be the proper amount to get you bounding out of the sack and doing jigs. I do understand that, at this point, you may be tempted to say, "eighteen hours". And truth is, after cutting this area of your life so short for so long, you might need a few round-the-clockers (meals airlifted to your bedroom) to start off. For this purpose, use the average number you think you'd like after you hit some sort of equilibrium.'

Now keep subtracting the following amounts:

- Time you <u>actually</u> spend each week at work – on the job or volunteering
- Amount of commute time – both directions multiplied by the number of days you work in a week. Allow for heavy traffic and missed buses
- Time you should, or would, like to spend with your children and/or pets over a week
- Time you would like to spend with your partner/spouse
- Time it would take to keep up with all your friends as you would like to, or as you now do
- Time you should spend on physical exercise
- Time you do, or should, spend on house chores: shopping, washing, repairs

---

[43] Exercise adapted from: *Enough is Enough* by Carol Orsborn, 1991. New World Library.

- Time for you to look good: having you hair cut, shaving or make-up, showers, drying your hair everyday
- Time for catching up and staying up to date with your reading
- Time for treats: walking in the county, walking the dog, etc
- Time to help your children to do their homework, taking them to school, visiting parents, administration for the family, going to church
- Time spent finding and booking baby sitters
- Time for anything else you do in your life -holidays, birthdays, phone calls, etc

You may find once you have subtracted what you do, and what you want to do but do not get around to doing, your number may turn negative. It is this kind of week lived for 52 weeks each year over many years that leads to you feeling temporally exhausted. A faulty sense of time is one that believes it is possible to continue stretching clock time indefinitely, and refuses to see that there are only 168 hours in the week.

We can't wait for anybody or anything
When we have to keep running mentally, physically, or both waiting is not an option. We talked earlier about the sense of entitlement that we feel with our pressured schedules, when we act in the world as if we had a God-given right not to be kept waiting. If you work with 2 computers and one is slower than the other you will recognise this sign. When you are waiting for the slow computer to connect with the Internet, you suddenly understand the reason for the findings that more and more employees attack their computers at work. Even though today we achieve speeds of communication that are quite remarkable, we still get impatient when that colleague does not reply to our email within the hour.

We have also lost our sense of the gap between wanting something and getting it, as an advert for a credit card told us a while ago: 'Access takes the waiting out of wanting'. The gap between desire and fulfilment of that desire is ever smaller. We will not wait. We have become the 'me, right Now!' generation. That there might be a problem with 'the wanting' or with 'the right now' is rarely challenged.

Important people don't wait, we hire those of lesser status to wait for us.[44] Our cleaner waits in for the sofa delivery. The valet parks our car and brings it to us as we will not wait for a parking space.

The periods of time we are willing to wait become shorter and shorter, so just about everything in life has an element of frustration for us because we cannot wait. This is reinforced by a society that lives on credit. So it is quite literally true that we have to wait for less and less, so long as we keep working to pay those credit cards, and this requires us to keep running faster and faster to get those tasks done. This means that our grasp of the future is becoming marginal. We have developed the idea that we can have the future right now for everything and, even more than that, that we are somehow entitled to have the future right now without consequences.

In business, we are starting to become aware of the problem of overactive managers.[45] So we run master classes on 'How to wait and take time to think'. In these classes we learn that we work well when we learn to wait to excel. The assumption here is that we slow down, but only so that we can then speed up again. We assume that fast is good. Here's an extract from one of my interviews: 'I read this article. It was an article about helping people with their energy around leadership, and it had this phrase in it, it was extolling the benefits of taking strategic pauses and it just amused me. Somehow in the life that we lead, we can't just stop. We have to take strategic pauses. It was rather like when they did that work on sleep, and napping was good for you, then it became a power nap. So now I am going to have a strategic pause. And there was no sense of irony about this in the article, that is what amused me.'

We feel Trapped in an empty present

We have little sense of a future, and no time for our past. This experience has been described to me as one of living in an empty present, when the present is understood as the 'future now' and the past not valued and forgotten. The world of business does seem to exist in an ahistorical context according to Joanne Ciulla: 'The

---

[44] In *The Geography of Time* by Robert Levine, 1997. Basic Books.
[45] In 'Waiting to excel'. *People Management*, August 29, 2002.

problem with management fads is that they are often uncritical and ahistorical.' She thinks that because of this management theorists continually discover the same things about work, and are just as delighted each time they do so.[46] This highlights the danger of having a faulty time sense. Those who cannot remember the past are condemned to repeat it.[47]

On the radio[48] the other morning the presenters were talking to the wives of two men who had had severe inflammation of the brain, and had been left with amnesia. One of them had lost all memory of his adult life and thought he was 14 years old. He got frustrated and angry when he looked in the mirror, he did not recognise 'that old man in the mirror'. Over the years he had been able to create new memories, and although he had a gap in his history he could function more normally as new memories were being created. The second man was stuck in a permanent now. He had no memory of the past and could not create new memories. His wife had to stop visiting him at the hospital, because he could remember that he loved her, but not what their life together had been like. Each time she saw him she created an emotional roller coaster in his mind. He felt that each time was the first time he had seen her for a lifetime, even though only 24 hours might have passed. Even more poignantly, his wife talked about her husband's diary. It had page after page of times crossed out: 'I woke up at 6.00, 7.00, 8.15, 8.30...9.00...' the frustration of each morning was more than she could bear to watch. This was a striking example of what it means to truly live in the present with no sense of past or future, or in other words, a hell on earth.

An extreme example, but one that shows us the consequences of continuing to disconnect the present moment from our past and future. The pace of our Now is such that it has outstripped our ability to imagine what might be, so we feel nothing is sacred. We also fail to value what was, so we feel ungrounded. We attach no value to

---

[46] J. Ciulla. Op cit. Page 140.
[47] George Santayana.
[48] The program was part of the Radio 4 'Between Ourselves' series entitled 'Amnesia'. It was broadcast at 11.15am on Sunday 28th July, 2002 and repeated the following Friday (August2nd) at 9.00am. The Radio 4 producer was Sara Lefroy-Owen. The two women featured were Christine Howell and Deborah Wearing.

experience; we are pronounced 'past it' at a younger and younger age. This is not a reflection on ability. It is a political decision that portrays the young as more flexible – by which perhaps we mean more compliant. They can, therefore, be more easily shaped to achieve the short-term profit goals of our organisations. Embedded in this lack of valuing the past is an ever-growing sense that our present is only about surface understanding and interactions, without the depth of the long-term.

We give more rather than take less

We have no time available for attending to others, and so try instead to give more to others. We give more money or material goods. I have no time to give to the hospice so I give a donation each month. I would like to visit old people but I have no time so I give money to Age Concern. I feel concern for the developing world and think about ways in which I could give money to the right charity to help them because they have so much less than we do, and I would like them to have as much as I do. This seems benign and almost a good side effect of my lack of time, but only if my actions are decontextualised from the economic reality of the world. We could not have as much as we do in the industrialised world if the developing world were no longer the developing world. The earth could not support the level of consumption this would entail. We know this at some level, but are too temporally exhausted to care; it is so much easier to sign a cheque to relieve the guilt. This is like the charity that plants trees to make up for the pollution we create when we use cars and planes. We pay the money to the charity and continue polluting the earth as we take our holidays.

Consider the alternative. The economist Wolfgang Sachs[49] defines justice not as the wealthy giving more, but as the wealthy taking less. He tells the story of the salmon that the Germans like to eat at dinner parties. Others in Europe eat salmon too, it's just that he is German. The consumption of this salmon in Germany is so high it is farmed in unsustainable ways. However, whilst the pleasant activity of eating salmon at a dinner party is happening in Germany, the negative

---

[49] I heard him at a conference held in London by Schumacher College, 2000.

environmental impact is happening in the Southern coast of Chile, where the feed for salmon farms is manufactured. We believe that we can keep taking more if we try to give more to the poor, he said. This is never going to achieve the stated impact of the developing world being as rich as we are. We have to accept that the only way to achieve the stated desire of helping the developing world is by us taking a little less each day. I wonder how my life would be different if I made my lifestyle choices through the criterion of taking less rather than giving more. Instead, I notice how often I give presents instead of working less and 'spending' more time with my family.

We are not very good with discomfort

I am walking in the country with a friend and have decided to wear my trainers for a short walk before lunch. It starts to rain heavily. The ground becomes soft and muddy, my trainers get soaked and I get very grumpy. My friend tries to make light of it but I will not have it. My feet are soggy, cold and I just hate everybody. As I focus on my discomfort and bad mood I hear him in the distance: 'You are not good with discomfort, are you?' I wish this were just a comment on my intolerance for wet shoes, but I believe it reflects a wider truth about our culture, that we are victims of comfort.

This discomfort is a sign of a faulty time sense because the lack of connection with our body and nature leads us to want to insulate ourselves from anything that distracts us from chasing deadlines. We have insulated ourselves from natural life so much that the effects on our health are clear. Since 1945 western populations have been getting weaker. For example, in 1960, the army had 140 recruits for every 100 places it offered, but by 1994 seventy people out of one hundred were being failed on physical grounds. The pasteurisation of milk in 1953 marked the end of many common illnesses, particularly tuberculosis. It also marked the start of a sharp decline in the general health of the population, as milk was a source of bacteria that strengthen the immune system. Men today have less than 50% of the sperm count they had in 1945. Oestrogen in our food, which has a number of harmful health effects, may only be partially responsible for this drop. We have become allergic to harmless things in our environment, as antibacterial sprays kill more and more bacteria in our homes, and our immune system no longer works so hard. Our clean lives cause us harm.

Television, central heating, the widespread use of cars and all things we label progress are increasing. Progress is aimed at increasing our comfort levels, yet contributes to a worsening of the general standard of health. We are a weakening species, removed from our origins and the natural environment where we thrived. We have moved away from correctness and expectations. The continuum of our species is broken. We have instead multimillion-dollar industries of exercise and health programs, which try in vain to stop us from getting fatter and fatter. Meanwhile, the food industries try to make us consume more by selling us bigger and bigger portions for a few cents more – a habit that has taken off in America and is known as 'biggie sizing'. Mad TV jokes that Americans are now asking: 'Can I fat ass that?' Overweight and desperate to shed a few pounds, we park as close to the health club as we can, in case it rains.

We 'do' Nature vicariously on the television. There are a number of programmes about living in discomfort. We have 'Big Brother' in which participants have to show they can live without TV and contact from the outside world. Interestingly, they do not have to do without alcohol and cigarettes. We then have 'Celebrity Big Brother', where B-list TV personalities are put through their paces for several weeks going without normal life. Then we have 'The Victorian Household' where a family agrees to live as families did over 100 years ago. There is also 'Surviving the Iron Age' and many others. The popularity of these shows has made TV channels a great deal of money. We take our discomfort third hand whilst watching TV. If we are really brave, we take an uncomfortable holiday in the form of a survival weekend.[50] 'Have you any idea how much wood and effort it requires to maintain a smouldering fire through a cold wet night?' the writer of this article on wild weekends complains. She adds, 'It is amazing how slow a day can go when everything you do is geared to keep yourself alive'.

I wonder if the trend for this kind of experience on television and in real life has something to do with us being aware that our

---

[50] Quotes from 'A wild weekend', *The Observer*, 26 August 2001.

discomfort with discomfort is a great disadvantage to our ability to live well? For years I believed in my right not to have to experience such discomfort. Success to me meant that I could create a life that deleted all experience I disliked, and highlighted all that I liked. Success was a cut and paste job on life. I did not have time to waste doing life maintenance jobs. I never thought success defined in this way could lead me to a future where I could become one of the 'pre-cogs' responsible for 'pre-crime' in the future depicted by 'The Minority Report'. All my life maintenance carried out by others and by machines to enable me to just think whilst lying in a pool of water all day...a life?

If comfort is avoidance of pain and discomfort, then we have to control life. We have to consume more and more to create the kind of environment where we can cushion ourselves from life. This means yet more temporal exhaustion is caused by our need for comfort.

> *'The modern world was eroded into its current form, by the overwhelming undertow of the power of comfort. Humans may have aspired to greatness in their talk or in their dreams, but the only life most of them genuinely craved was the easier one. So through the ages they worked, researched, and more than occasionally struggled, paradoxically, to find ways to make life more comfortable. But comparatives never make good targets: if you want an easy life, you will know when you've got it, but if you set your sights on an easier life, then there will always be further to go. Our changes stopped being improvements long ago: now they are irresistible shuffles towards the inevitable rigor mortis of utopian comfort.'*
> David Whiteland [51]

We are terrified of the future

We have lost our sense of how the past has created our present, 'the destruction of the past, or rather of the social mechanisms that link one's contemporary experience to that of earlier generations, is

---

[51] From *The Book of Pages* by David Whiteland. Ringpull Press, 2000. www.bookofpages.com.

one of the most characteristic and eerie phenomena of the late 20th Century. Most young men and women at the century's end grow up in a sort of permanent present lacking any organic relation to the public past of the times they live in'.[52]

This phenomenon has led us to live in a permanent present lacking any organic relation to a public future. Maybe the pace of change is such, says Madeleine Bunting[53], that it has overtaken our imagination. We are scared of the unknown, and because we can't imagine life in 2035, we feel fear. Or, she ventures, there may be a second reason: 'We are utterly self-obsessed. We think neither of our ancestors nor of our descendants. We have developed the most self-centred culture in the history of humanity.' She believes that our society has as its sole focus the creation of wealth and entertainment, and that we live to have as much of both as we can without delay. In our permanent present we can only feel terror for the future. I think our self-centred culture causes the pace of change, and that this self-centred culture is, in turn, caused by a faulty sense of time. The lack of connection with our past and our future causes the fear. We can make a choice to actively learn to reconnect, and notice how that changes the quality of our lives. In so doing, we may discover that we can no longer make self-centred choices, and this may be precisely why we choose instead not to look forward or back.

The trouble with the future is that we die there. This is the biggest uncertainty of all, and the most dreaded when your life coheres only in self-serving goals. Enter the Botox babes[54] in an article that explores the new trend for pretty 'twenty somethings' who choose to improve their looks with an injection. The article interviews several young women who are using botox injections and chemical fillers to iron out wrinkles. The treatments are also being used 'as a preventive strike, against what they see as the inevitable'. The reasons they give for needing the treatment are noticing wrinkles around the eyes, long working hours, driving and squinting at night, and the belief that they will never need a face-lift if they do this now. They talk about how

---

[52] Eric Hobsbawm, *The Age of Extremes*', 1999. Quoted in M. Bunting's 'Don't Look Now – This Is Your Future', *The Guardian*, January 21, 2100.
[53] In 'Don't Look Now – This Is Your Future', *The Guardian*, January 21, 2100.
[54] *Evening Standard*, Tuesday, 26 February, 2002.

2. A faulty sense of time 79

these treatments can nip the problem of wrinkles in the bud. There is no sense of irony in the article, and the assumption that it is possible to stop the ageing process goes unchallenged. The illusion that we can control time and nature has reached delusional heights in the young. They are working long hours to earn the money to cover up the signs that they are working long hours. Fear of death makes us act in very unhealthy ways. We are always dissatisfied with life as it is because we mistakenly believe that we have the capacity to want (and get) perfection in wrinkle free faces, or in enlightened minds.

> *"We should not complain' said the first leaf gently, 'We've outlived many many others.' 'Have I changed much?' asked the second leaf shyly but determinedly. 'Not in the least' the first leaf assured her. 'You only think so because I got to be so yellow and ugly. But it is different in your case.' 'You are fooling me' the second leaf said. 'Hush' said the other leaf, and kept silent herself, for she was too troubled to talk any more. They both were silent. Hours passed. A moist wind blew cold and hostile through the treetops. 'Ah, now,' said the second leaf, 'I...' Then her voice broke off. She was torn from her place and spun down. Winter had come.'*
> Felix Saltern[55]

We experience Learning fatigue

We know that whatever we learn today will be out of date, obsolete almost as soon as we have mastered it, including computer packages, our business strategy and even our relationships with our team. We have made a virtue of changing jobs faster and faster. We sell the virtue of life long learning, and hold people responsible for not learning fast enough. But in reality learning takes time, and learning difficult things we know will be out of date sooner than we can master them can lead to a feeling of helplessness. We are driven to feel that we can only be successful if we can keep increasing the rate at which

---

[55] In *Bambi* by Felix Saltern, 1999. Atheneum Books.

we learn and dispose of things, people and plans. 'More thinking' applied to our learning speed.

The old-young ones
One of the organisations I work with is in the Internet business. They are still succeeding at the time of writing in spite of the many casualties in that sector over recent years. I was working with the senior team to help them with their personal planning skills, or time management by any other name. I ran focus groups to find out how people in an industry that is the epitome of speed perceived its impact on people. I asked: 'What have you learnt about ways to handle the speed of change in your industry? What impact does it have on your life?' A summary of their answers follows.

- My focus is to gain experience for the next stage
- I have learnt about the transient nature of the IT industry
- The aim is to gain expertise – learn and move on
- We are constantly doing different and new things
- Enjoy what I do now, life is too short
- Do as much as I can as quickly as possible to get out of it as quickly as I can
- Days go so fast, I often think 'May already'?
- Work impacts more and more on your personal life
- Lots of learning, the speed of it is frightening
- Contracts last for just a few months, insecurity is the name of the game – who dares to really push their ideas? We are mostly afraid to make mistakes
- If I don't perform, I'm out. I will not say 'you are wrong' to my boss, will I?
- Money was in the ideas, but the ideas have slowed down now
- Not easy to make money
- My life suffers badly from the speed of change
- No time for health, friends
- I miss out a lot on the rest of my life
- Sometimes it gives me a buzz, I like the buzz
- I feel pressured to learn new things
- We don't take time to make things really work

2. A faulty sense of time

- I know that what I do today will be pointless next year
- Positive change would come if people started to care about people and product rather than the speed of changing the technology
- Are we ourselves making it go faster with our motivation to get out of it quickly and make lots of money quickly?
- The industry encourages people to look at themselves as commodities rather than people
- I feel like I sold my soul to the devil
- A lot of people are choosing to come into the industry because of the reward not because of a passion
- If I had all the time in the world I would be more likely to do what I want right now, rather than wait until I am 30
- The boom will end, level out. This gives us all a sense of urgency
- So many ambitious people in it
- It is not a stable situation
- The dream is to create the situation of the early days when a 14 year old could come up with a good idea and become a millionaire

The 14-year-old was playing with ideas for ideas' sake. The speed expected today is such that the slow time needed for idea generation cannot be taken. So all that can be done is to come up with quick improvements to existing ideas. From the comments above it may appear that these people are at the end of their careers. They are in senior positions, and they are also only in their twenties, but they expressed an overwhelming sense of exhaustion, and emphasised the fact that nothing is ever finished. They say that the technology is not really exploited. 'We are just hooked on how quickly we can make it change'. I was sad to see a group of young and talented people talking as if they had just lived too long and learnt too much too fast. I felt no sense of play and curiosity coming from them, just a sense of pressure and a need to get rich quick before the dream fades. With such a strong and constant fear of 'losing it all', how could they do anything other than run faster than their competitors?

So, if you have a sense of dread at the news that that new version of your office software is being installed on Monday, please don't dismiss it as unimportant. Learning fatigue is a valid sign that our sense of time is faulty. Of course learning is a valuable skill. However, when we learn but know that our learning has the lifespan of a packet of crisps, experiencing learning fatigue is inevitable.

A faulty sense of time leads us to pursue unsustainable lives. We crave I-thou connections with those around us. However, our addiction to clock time has made us feel disconnected from each other and life. Life needs coherent entanglements to be a full life. If instead of trying to fix ourselves in relation to clock time, we focus on developing a healthy time sense we will find the peace of mind we look for, and then we will no longer just wait to excel, we will excel at waiting. This is possible if we connect with correct rather than corrective action.

LIVED TIME

Lived Time

'It is a mistake, this extreme precision, this orderly and military progress; a convenience, a lie. There is always deep below it, even when we arrive punctually at the appointed time with our white waistcoats and polite formalities, a rushing stream of broken dreams, nursery rhymes, street cries, half-finished sentences and sights – elm trees, willow trees, gardeners sweeping, women writing – that rise and sink...'
Virginia Woolf[56]

As I stare at the spider's web, visible only because it is a particular time in the morning and only because there is a particular kind of weather, I start to believe in synchronicity. I had laughed cynically 24 hours earlier when reading a description of somebody looking at spider webs on the other side of the world in a different time zone. I sat on a bench in my garden and suddenly caught sight of something glistening in a pine tree. As I got closer I saw many of these webs in the same tree. I stared. As I drank my morning coffee, I played with my perception. I could focus my eyes in such a way that there was 'nothing' but empty space between the branches, or I could 'see' the webs in the 'empty' space. Looking for what is not there. This was my introduction to a morning in lived time. No clocks, but I noticed the birds talked to each other in many languages. No deadlines, but I noticed that I could hear the tree speaking too. No sense of time outside of me, but a sense of events happening with my body being just one element in a present that contained the whole of life. I engaged in conversations with my neighbour, my mother, with my breathing, the birds and the trees. I checked the webs again. They had seemingly disappeared; I could no longer see them with my eyes, though I could touch them and destroy them with my fingers. Time had moved on, time for lunch.

---

[56]   In *Time and Reality: Studies in Contemporary Fiction*, by Margaret Church, 1963. University of North Carolina Press.

3. Lived time

Lived time challenges the way in which clock time forces us to structure our perceptions. It is a kind of time where each individual is merely part of a huge system, where the centre of gravity moves back to the earth where it belongs. We are so used to the centre of gravity being within us. 'Am I self-centred? Or is it just me?' A logo written on a T-shirt I saw a long time ago.

> **'Meanwhile, man, precisely as the one so threatened, exalts himself and postures as lord of the earth. In this way the illusion comes to prevail that everything man encounters exists only insofar as it is his construct. This illusion gives rise in turn to one final illusion: it seems as though man everywhere and always encounters only himself'**
> Martin Heidegger[57]

Humans have been fascinated with time since the beginning of time. We have so many kinds of time, each highlighting a particular aspect of human experience. So we have meditation time, wild time, play time, life time, vampire time, Matrix time, skydiving time, hypnotic time, holiday time, work time, individual time, communal time, finite time, infinite time, TV time, space-time, subjective time, non-linear dreamtime, time-based art, Assyrian eternal time, Medieval European apocalyptic time, Indian cosmic cyclical time, African ancestral time, Native American episodic time, Mayan calendar time, creative time, each time highlighting different aspects of life. Each kind of time has its own pace, its own tempo, in the same way that each of us has our own unique inner sense of time that informs the choices we make in the events of our lives.

How far removed is this kind of time from the kind of time of the previous chapters. I notice also that the quality of language that describes one has efficiency as its purpose, while the kind of language that describes the other has description as its purpose. Lived time takes much longer than clock time to unfold. As Julius Thomas Fraser, the founder of The International Society for the Study of Time once

---

[57] Quoted in *The Spell of the Sensuous* by David Abram, 1996. Vintage.

said: 'Tell me what you think about time and I shall know what to think of you'. Our time is our life and our narrative; the theory we have about what time is and how we relate to it says less about time than it does about us.

Types of time

Kairos and Kronos
The Greeks originated the distinction between time that is independent of man (Kronos) praised for accuracy, and time that is embedded in the daily experience of man, such as harvests and feeding, (Kairos). Thus they distinguished between the god of time and the god of timing.

Polychronic and monochronic time
What kind of scheduler are you? The distinction between polychronic and monochronic time speaks to our preference for starting many things in parallel, or one thing at a time. We are encouraged to get good at polychronic time as it is supposed to allow us to achieve more in less time. Perhaps this has encouraged us to unlearn monochronic time to such an extent that we are unable to sit in the stillness of dedicating our attention fully to just one thing at a time.

Set up time and activity time
This distinction is about the time it takes to cogitate, think, reflect and ruminate on the best way to do something, versus the time it takes to actually do that thing. As a writer, I am always aware of this time distinction. Set up time for a chapter is always longer than the time it takes to write it. Organisations do not want to work with set up time, the hidden time of activity, and preparation for activity is often not considered work time at all. Set up time focuses us on the importance of absences. Creativity lives in set up time. We are often overloaded because of our lack of understanding of the need for set up time in our thinking.

3. Lived time

Divided and undivided time

Divided time is the kind of time you experience when you have to take a long train journey and you have to change 3 times. Undivided time is the kind of time you experience when you go on a 3 or 4 hours journey and the train has a mobile phone free zone! I love this kind of time because I finally have a name for the kind of time I used to love as a child in Argentina. We took our summer vacations in the North of the country. Nothing ever happened. We had 3 months in 'Smallville' Argentina, where all we could do was talk to friends and watch the world go by. I had such peace there, watching the skies at night for hours, and sitting outside with my friends at siesta time while the adults slept and there was even less going on.

Back to work here. We have got so used to divided time that we find undivided time boring and wasteful. We have become a world of grazers. You have seen the cow going from one bit of the field to another grazing. Grazers is a term used in the advertising world to describe our habit of not watching one channel, but of switching from one to the other every few seconds. Divided time is definitely the child of clock time.

Fast time and slow time

> '[We live in] a culture ignorant of the past and viciously refusing to plan for the future, not respecting the old, not cherishing the young. Its exports are adolescent; fast cars, fast food, fast talk, fast bucks, fast war. Fast in everything, puerile and premature, modern westernised cultures could never have produced the 'Kama Sutra', would never pause to consider the point of orgasm maintained for hours.'
> Jay Griffiths[58]

We have grown to believe that living on fast time is the same as being efficient, and that living in slow time is, at best, only needed to keep going faster and faster later. Slow time is also recommended for those

---

[58] In *Pip Pip*, 1999. Flamingo.

who want to work smarter not harder. The suggestion is not a change of ethos, just a change of technique to keep living in clock time.

The pursuit of fast time has become the Holy Grail of work. The practice of hot-desking in some large organisations is designed for people to produce on the go. There is no need to settle anywhere, as you can work on any available desk in any office in the country. I was told recently by a course participant, a senior manager in a financial organisation that all they are allowed is a small trolley on wheels that can move with them quickly to wherever they want to be in the building. An additional practice at the same organisation was what I came to call meetings to go; they conducted meetings standing up in order to get on with the task quickly and not linger. God forbid they might be found doing that most abominable of human activities, having a relaxed conversation. What I found most shocking was that these practices were talked about in a positive way, as a good way not to waste any time and be efficient.

Clock time and event time

When I started the research for this book I was surprised by the fact that clock time is relatively new in existence, although I knew in my head that time pieces were a human invention. I had even read Longitude, which tells the story of John Harrison, who dedicated his life to the search for a perfect timekeeper. However, when I really started to imagine life without clock time I was barely able to do so. There was a time when people agreed to meet 'at the time the cows go out grazing'. There was a time when there was only local time and train schedules were a nightmare so they invented rail time in America. There was a time when human activity served as a measure of time rather than the other way around. Some people call this event time, what I call lived time in this book. Standard clock time came to America in 1884. I found that difficult to imagine, and was surprised by how relatively recently clock time had been invented.

I have now learnt that there still are cultures that work on event time. There are also cultures that work on dual time, exemplified by the phrases 'hora mexicana' and 'hora inglesa', used by Mexicans who live on the Mexican side of the American border and commute to

America for work. Certain peoples in Africa keep 'coconut-time' when they play sport, and do clock time when they work. Coconut time is a bucket of water, a coconut shell with a small hole in the middle and the time units are the time it takes for the coconut to get full of water. I imagine the sports teams behind the scenes arguing whose turn it is to turn the coconut over! Event time is the kind of time that keeps humans involved with the process of marking time. Clock time dispenses with humans, and technology has created a clock in Boulder, Colorado, which will not lose a second in over a million years. Whilst I know that accurate timing is important to things like satellites, I begrudge the kind of money that must have been spent creating this perfect clock.

> *The gods confound the man who first found out*
> *How to distinguish hours – confound him, too,*
> *Who in this place set up a sundial*
> *To cut and hack my days so wretchedly*
> *Into small pieces! When I was a boy,*
> *My belly was my sundial-one more sure,*
> *Truer, and more exact than any of them.*
> *This dial told when 'twas proper time*
> *To go to dinner, when I ought to eat;*
> *But nowadays, why even when I have,*
> *I can't fall to unless the sun gives leave,*
> *The town's so full of these confounded dials.*

(Written two thousand years ago by the Roman playwright Plautus[59])

Understanding lived time

As you saw in the distinctions above there are many ways to slice time. To deepen our understanding of lived time it is useful to look at phenomenology, because phenomenologists are not interested in looking at whether our inner sense of time matches up with scientific time as measured by a measuring device. They want to understand

---

[59] Quoted in *Timelock* by Ralph Keyes, 1991. Harper Collins Inc.

our subjective experience of time. This is different from approaches that try to convince me that what my senses tell me does not make sense, and that I need the clock in Boulder to know if I am hungry. I want to pay attention to a group of people who believe that humans could do with a little more humility, that maybe, just maybe, we cannot create an objective finished blueprint of the world because we are not able to stand outside our experience. I turn to the work of David Abram[60] in what follows.

We have developed a conception of our body built through studies of corpses. The anatomised corpse creates our sense of ourselves as a physical entity. Just as with clock time, medicine has reduced and broken down our body to such an extent that specialists now know a great deal about very little. Just as we break up every human activity further and further to allow us to 'do more' within the same snapshot of time, we have broken up the human body further and further in the hope of finally discovering the definitive blueprint.

Things are not quite working though. Hard as we try to perceive our bodies as separate systems, we crave the experience of being treated as one entity. Evidence of this in health is the popularity of holistic therapies for the treatment of many illnesses. James Hillman[61] believes that we should treat all events and objects in our world as if they were alive, thereby connecting us to a soul world or anima mundi. He says, we should treat: 'each thing animate or inanimate, natural and manmade, as if it were alive, requiring what each living thing requires above all else: careful attention to its properties, their specific qualities'. However, we do not treat things and events as if they were alive, we even treat people as if they were inanimate things. Hence we crave careful attention to our unique properties. Holistic therapies give us this deep attention, conventional medicine breaks us up into smaller and smaller parts with the whole getting less and less attention.

---

[60] Thanks to David Abram and *The Spell of the Sensuous* (Vintage, 1996) for helping me crystallise my thinking for this section. His book should be mandatory reading to each being born on this earth. It is inspired and inspiring. I will draw from him a great deal in what follows.

[61] In *Kinds of Power – A guide to its intelligent uses*. James Hillman, 1995. Currency Doubleday.

Mae-Wan Ho[62] comments on how she argues with colleagues who tell her that something is not 'real' until it has been measured on a dead body. Her work on the biology of living organisms shows us beautiful pictures of how all organisms require both a slow and a fast pace simultaneously to sustain life. I write and talk fast, but I digest my lunch slowly. Modern medicine knows nothing about our bodies as living systems, but, for example, acupuncture does. Western medicine now uses acupuncture, but cannot explain how it works within its reductionistic models. Reductionism leads us to ignore the wisdom of our bodies, and can make us become dependent on chemicals. In modern western medicine the distinction between addiction and prescription has become quite blurred.

Abram offers us an alternative view of our bodies. This includes our breathing bodies, and seeing the world as it is experienced 'in its felt immediacy'. He sees mind not as an object, but as an epiphenomenon of our body perceiving the fluidity of the moment. This idea gives us a way of thinking about time as lived time – where the focus is not explanation of experience, but a description of it, where our role is not to control nature but to give it a voice.

Phenomenology tells us that 'everything we do, including explanation, is rooted in this life-world'[63]. We experience inner conflict in the argument between our mental constructs, which tell us it is possible to get an objective blueprint, and our bodily precepts, which tell us that even blueprints have to be created and perceived by somebody.

Merleau Ponty tells us our intellect is an elaboration of the world. The self is our body, since there would be no experience without it. We live in perceptual reciprocity with the world. This perceptual reciprocity is a silent conversation without language that keeps us open to the world. We perceive, and are perceived by the world. So the world is in some way animate, like Hillman's Anima Mundi. This web-like system of connections is elaborated in our intellectual abstract thought. Abram comments on the fact that we are never able to perceive an object completely. So if we look at a cup on a

---

[62] From a talk at a Schumacher College conference, in London, 2001.
[63] Husserl. Quoted in *Spell of the Sensuous* p60.

table we can only see one side and cannot see the inside. If we pick it up and look inside we cannot see the outside's bottom. Our senses need to 'throw themselves beyond the information given' in order to make sense of the world. This gets elaborated in our mental world into what we call our imagination.

This is how we participate in the world, and this participatory flux cannot be suspended. The participatory flux makes sense. It is the essence of lived time. Our senses diverge from our bodies and converge on the perceived thing. We need that convergence to feel at home. This coming together in the life-world is how our senses make sense, and how our minds make meaning. 'This body is a form destined to the world...[an] open circuit that completes itself only in things, in others, in the encompassing earth'.

As we move away from nature, we increasingly become convinced we are just cause and not effect. The final illusion is complete, and we think because we only encounter ourselves, there is only ourselves. I believe that in retreating to seeing as true only that which we have created in our image, we are also developing a faulty time sense that keeps us constantly searching for peace of mind in clock time.

Abram suggests that we are designed to be part of a system that has great diversity. The earth and its inhabitants create patterns humans did not devise therefore they surprise us. The patterns are never quite the same, never quite repeating. This means our senses stay alive to the present moment in order to make sense of the surprises. This is what feeds our soul. As we move away from nature and retreat into a world of mass-produced objects, which are always the same, and predictable because they are patterns of our design, we keep searching for an element of surprise. We have a need to acquire more and more in order to keep our senses active and alive.

Our bodies are really looking for the surprise of the earth, says Abram, but we have disconnected from it, and we look in the wrong place. It is the same with time. We keep tinkering with clock time to help us make sense of our disjointed and incoherent lives, and we keep getting the same results back, more incoherence and more breaking up. Lived time is about looking in the right place, in your senses, and your body. It is about seeing the world as the same 'stuff' as me in my body. This is what Merleau Ponty called the flesh of the world, subject and object as 'reversible aspects of a common animate element'.

Abram argues that our role within the system is not to control it, but to give voice to it. Language plays a key part in helping us renew our reciprocity with the earth. As we use words, Abram tells us: 'we speak and the world speaks within us'. Language is not viewed as a formal system, which is readily detachable from the act of living our lives. How could it be that? We have developed such a view of language because we live in times when, Abram tells us: 'the fresh creation of meaning has become a rare occurrence, a time when people speak in ready-made conventional ways...a time when meaning has become impoverished'. We have lost the ability to speak sentences that hold thought, for to speak thoughtfully and with depth takes longer than to speak in clichés.

Abram names and describes the experience I have each time I ring a call centre and try to establish a human conversation with the person on the other end of the phone. Language becomes impoverished because we are disconnected from lived experience. If we view language as a system of difference, where words are defined not in themselves but in relation to one another, we see that it is what Abram calls: 'a thoroughly interdependent matrix, a web-work wherein each term has meaning only in relation to other terms within the system'. In other words, meaning lies in the interval between the terms. He calls this the absences, whereby words that are not spoken are as important as the words that are, because they find meaning in relation to them.

Just as with language, the nature of lived time can only be defined as a web-work where all the parts are defined in relation to each other. Our physical being gives us the model to map onto our conception of time. We can choose to see time as a detached formal system – clock time, or we can see it as a web of lived experience that keeps us grounded in our sensory world. As clock time tore us away from the fabric of events in our lives, we lost our sense of time. We lost our senses, in a real and not a metaphorical way. We became guests in our own existence.

How could this happen? Abram looks at where in our history this separation between world and word could have originated. This diversion is worthwhile, to help us make sense of our current state of clock addiction. A long time ago we did not have an alphabet. Our writing systems consisted of drawings that represented the world around us. You saw a cow and you drew a stylised picture of a cow. If you wanted to express the fact that you wanted many cows then you might go to a sacred place and draw pictures of many cows, to ask the gods to bring you good fortune. Our signs were tied to the world around us. Then somebody had the idea that you could use the sign of a cow under a tree to represent the idea of 'finding shelter from the sun'. So you now used the same sign, but it no longer referred directly to the cows. You could use the sign as a note on a rock for your pal who had gone hunting: 'I've gone for a nap'. He returns, sees the 'note' and knows where to go to find you. The signs are still tied to the environment, but one step removed. During this time people are still using words to communicate verbally, and pictures only on rocks. What has not happened yet is the translation of words onto rock.

Then along comes somebody else, who works out that the written signs for 'bee' and 'leaf' can be used to stand for the sound in spoken language of the word 'belief'. You now have made the first step towards becoming independent of the environment, and can now start to write phonetically. This means that writing becomes what you are doing right now as you read these words. You sound out the marks of ink on the page and 'your senses go beyond the information given', as Abram says, to create in your mind words, sounds, images and feelings. Thus we learn to find our sense of coherence in the written page, through our own signs and not the rest of nature.

Abram blames it on our alphabet. A move which I love because it makes me stop and think about the negative consequences of one of the things I love most in the whole world, words. Our phonetic alphabet based on sounds and not things, travels to Greece. Because 'things' are no longer necessary to discuss concepts, it is now possible to adapt our conceptual system in such a way that we can now discuss 'truth' and 'freedom' independent of the actual lived examples of these words.

This also makes it possible to freeze time in the written word. So where it was once necessary to hold knowledge and wisdom in oral stories, it now becomes possible to write these stories down and reflect on them. Our ability for self-reflection is thus born. We now have the ability to read about times past. We can reflect on places we have never visited. The dislocation between my body and my place is now complete. The impact of this is that our intellect has flourished, but that we have lost our sense of being the flesh of the world.

This is a simplified and light-hearted look at Abram's thesis. His research is impeccable and the story telling compelling. The purpose of this diversion is to stress that the concepts that we take as given, as true, are responses to particular developments in our lived experience. The ability to make meaning from marks of ink on a piece of paper is something that once upon a time would have been considered the work of Satan.

Plato had something to say about the possible impact of writing: 'If men learn this, it will implant forgetfulness in their souls; they will cease to exercise memory because they rely on that which is written, calling things to remembrance no longer from within themselves, but by means of external marks'. He stressed the importance of using writing only as a reminder of things that we know through lived experience. Abram points out that in spite of his cautions, Plato was already steeped in the distinction between the abstract and the concrete. Abram believes that sensory involvement with new tools changes our perceptions and thoughts. We do not know how computers and the Internet are affecting our thoughts, but we can 'be sure that the shapes of our consciousness are shifting in tandem with the technologies that engage our senses'.[64]

Here is a small example of the process we are talking about. The sign for 'water' in ancient Hebrew was a curvy line that looked like a wave. This curvy line is the precursor of our present day letter 'M'. So even today there are some tenuous links between our signs and our world.

We have only the benefit of hindsight to create a plausible story about how we have lost our reciprocal connection with nature and transferred it to our man-made signs. We even have a villain in our story with the power of the alphabet to distance us from the world. The alphabet got us reading, and then we got lost in our own signs. We hear marks of ink on the page rather than the trees. A healthy

---

[64] Ibid. Page 115.

sense of time is one that uses more than just man-made signs to make sense of time through our body.

It may now be clear that our taken-for-granted assumptions about time are just that; working assumptions that we have put in place, often unconsciously, to help us lead a more fruitful life. I hope you now feel more open to believing in the possibility of an experience of time that does not leave you feeling out of breath, metaphorically or literally, at the end of each day.

There are those[65] who believe that we can only understand through metaphor, and that our body provides us with the source for our ability to understand any concept. This is like Merleau-Ponty saying that our thoughts are an elaboration of the creativity of the physical world. So whilst Abram made connections between our perception and the earth in his analysis, George Lakoff and Mark Johnson link our perception with our abstract thought.

I will end this chapter on lived time with a review of Lakoff and Johnson's work because I believe it can dislodge further the received view of time as a linear process located outside of ourselves. Time, they argue, is an abstract notion that can only be understood metaphorically in terms of other human activities. They reject the view that the mental realms of space and time are independent from experience. They produce compelling linguistic evidence for their argument that even mathematics is understood through living metaphors, and cannot be made sense of independently of these. They believe that metaphorical understanding provides the ground for making sense of all abstract human endeavours. The analysis of language is used to provide evidence for their arguments within their field of work, cognitive linguistics. Their work shows that our understanding of time is not independent but tied to our body. We understand time as motion, as space, as events.

---

[65] What follows draws from the work of George Lakoff and Mark Johnson. They have been part of my life ever since I discovered their work when researching for my PhD. When I read their work I toggle between thinking it is sheer genius and Forrest Gump. Perhaps, when an idea is clearly and elegantly elucidated, we tend to think it obvious. Living on the edge of stupidity and genius, may just be the mark of remarkable people. The book where they analyse time is called *Philosophy in the Flesh* and it was published in 1999. As an introduction to their work read 'Metaphors we live by'. Published in 1980 by University of Chicago Press.

3. Lived time

We think of time as a succesive iteration of physical events

A sundial depends on the regular movement of the sun, and a clock depends on the regular and iterated motion of a pendulum. Some scientists believe we have an internal 'clock' in the form of an electrical pulse that is sent though the brain every 40 seconds or so. From this we can say that it is regular events that can be measured, and not time itself. The successive iterations of events stand for a given interval of time. Lakoff and Johnson believe that the basic properties of our concept of time are a consequence of the basic properties of events:

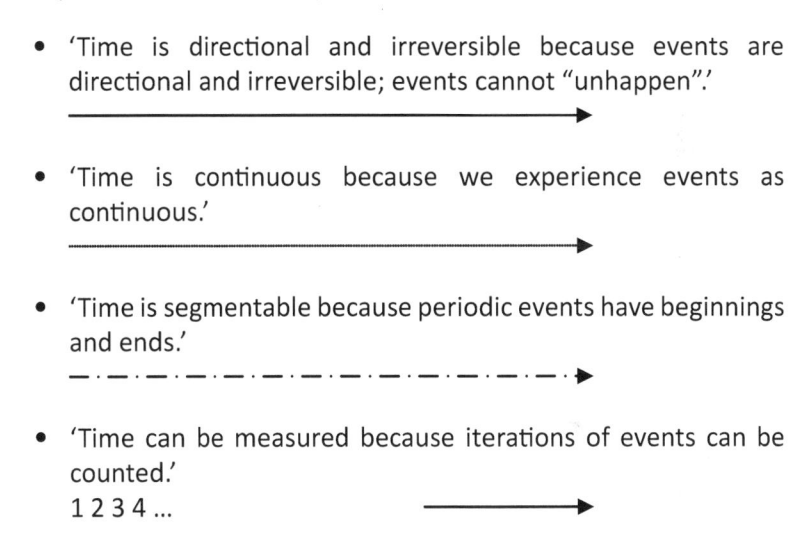

- 'Time is directional and irreversible because events are directional and irreversible; events cannot "unhappen".'
  ⟶

- 'Time is continuous because we experience events as continuous.'
  ⟶

- 'Time is segmentable because periodic events have beginnings and ends.'
  —·—·—·—·—·—·—·—·—·—▸

- 'Time can be measured because iterations of events can be counted.'
  1 2 3 4 … ⟶

We understand time because we perceive events and are able to notice patterns in events.

We think of time as movement in space

We move our bodies in relation to our surroundings. We define time in terms of our experience of moving in the world. We perceive motion directly; we perceive time indirectly through motion. Below we look at what language can tell us about the way we think.

- **Time orientation** – 'That's all behind us now.' 'Let's put that to the back of us.' 'We're looking ahead to the future.' 'He has a great future in front of him'.

When we use this kind of language we are talking about time. We are talking about how we orient ourselves in relation to time. Most of us think of the past as being behind, with the future being in front and the present located wherever we are in space. This may seem obvious and perhaps it is. However, there are cultures in South America that conceive of the future as 'behind them' because they have not seen it yet and the past and present 'in front of them' because it is what is already known. Psychologists who study the structure of subjective experience also propose that there are individual differences in the way we orient to time. What is certain is that we use the location of our body as a point of orientation for time constructs.

- **Moving Time** – 'The time will *come* when there are no more typewriters.' 'The time has long since *gone* when you could mail a letter for 3 cents.' 'The time for action *has arrived*.' 'Time is *flying by*.' 'The time for end-of-summer sales *has passed*.' 'The *deadline is approaching*.'

    Imagine that you are sitting on a train watching the world go by through the window. When we conceive of time moving it is like that. We are fixed in a location and from that vantage point we sense time 'go by'. It is as if temporal objects were going past us and the direction of motion was determined by the front of the temporal object. Time can *approach* and go *past* us. The mapping, how we link our perception and abstract thought, is like this: 'Time (abstract thought) is an object (concrete perception)' and 'the movement of objects is the passage of time'. There is another way in which we think of time as moving. We talk about the *flow* of time, where the structuring metaphor is that of a river flowing past us.

- **Moving observer** – 'There's going to be trouble *down the road*.' 'Will you be staying a *long* time or a *short* time?' 'What will be the *length* of his visit?' 'His visit to Russia *extended over* many years.' 'Let's spread the conference *over* two weeks.'

'The conference *runs from* the first *to* the tenth of the month.'
'We've *reached* June already.'
   Now imagine you are going for a walk along a favourite trail. Time is here conceptualised as a fixed landscape through which I, the observer, move. As I walk along each location I reach is a time, wherever the observer happens to be is the now, time passes as the observer moves and the distance covered is equated to the amount of time that has passed. I link the perception of covering a certain distance when I walk with the abstract idea of moving through time, which we call a mapping from the concrete to the abstract. This map is created to enable us to understand abstract concepts like time. As I continue walking I know that I am *getting close to* a particular location. We also say, I am *close to* that deadline.

Notice that whilst the last two organising metaphors are correctly used in our conversations about time, they are not consistent. Take the word 'pass'. I can say that 'time has passed', an example of the Moving Time metaphor. I can use the same verb to say 'I passed the time pleasantly', an example of the Moving Observer metaphor. Think of the verb *'Move ahead'*. As in 'Let's *move* the meeting *ahead* a week'. The verb fits both metaphors. If you have booked a meeting for Friday, next week, when do you think the meeting will be moved to? Think of words like *ooze, sneak, march and cascade,* they indicate motion. You can make up some sentences that talk about time using these verbs. As in 'the deadline was *marching towards* me like a brass band'. These are all further examples of the Moving Time metaphor, which are not used in everyday speech but which 'make sense' to us through the Moving Time metaphor.

   However, even if spatial expression helps us talk about time, there are inconsistencies and ambiguities. Everyday we move in the world in relation to things and people. These are categorised as 'motion situations' by researchers. Everyday we are aware of our bodily rhythms, the movement of clocks, and these are categorised as 'time-defining events'. We correlate time-defining events with motion situations, and thus have a way of talking about time that makes sense, in the literal sense. We say: 'San Francisco is half an hour from

Berkeley' – here time stands for distance. Or, 'I slept for fifty miles while she drove' – here distance stands for time.

We think of time as money

'You have some time *left*.' 'You've *used up* all your time.' 'I've got *plenty* of time to do that.' 'I don't have *enough* time to do that.' 'That *took* three hours.' 'He *wasted* an hour of my time.' 'I have to *budget* my time.' 'I *spent* too much time on that.' 'I've *invested* a lot of time on this project.' 'You don't use your time *profitably*.' 'That mistake resulted in a considerable *loss* of time.'

Our culture structures time through this metaphor so much that it has become reified in our institutions. The New Economics foundation has started a new initiative called 'Time Banks'. We talk about being money rich, but time poor. Time is a non-renewable resource that can be measured and used up. This is clock time, where the resource is time, which is used up by a person for a purpose. The resource of time has a value, and the purpose for which time is being used has a value too. God forbid we might waste time for a purpose that is not valuable.

Lakoff and Johnson say that we cannot deny that this metaphor is true in our culture, but this is not the only possible truth. We have so many institutions that reify time as money – we pay people by the hour worked, we budget time in appointment books, we have clocks, we have business hours, we have deadlines. How else would we create the urgency of clock time addiction if not by turning time into a limited non-renewable resource? But Lakoff and Johnson show us that not all cultures conceive of time this way.

For example, the Pueblo Indians cannot talk about not having enough time to do something. Their language only allows them to say: 'My path did not take me there' or ' I could not find a path to do that'. We talked earlier about the notion of 'Hora Mexicana' and 'Hora Inglesa' for those people that kept dual time. 'English time' (Hora Inglesa) is 'doing time' according to the 'time is money' metaphor. 'Mexican time' (Hora Mexicana) is doing time according to the 'Moving Observer metaphor'. There are people in the world, perhaps those who can live on 'coconut time', who cannot talk or think about time as something that can be bought, or is in short supply. There are more of these cultures than we care to admit, and the job of our global organisations has often been to import the idea that 'time is money' into their cultures. This disrupts the very fabric of their notions of time, and oftentimes, arrogantly mocks them for not seeing the absolute and indisputable truth that time IS money.

The cost of our reification of clock time is plain for all to see. Maybe it is time that we start reifying different metaphors for time in our world, rather than modelling ourselves on the clock. It is sad that the very thing that makes human beings so unique may also destroy us – our ability to absorb the conceptual until it becomes a perceptual reality, time IS money.

THE GREAT EMPLOYEE TIME ROBBERY

Employees across the nation this year will steal $150 billion worth of time from their jobs in what is termed by an employment specialist as the "deliberate and persistent abuse" of paid working hours.

The study, released by Robert Half International, Inc., reported that the theft of working time is America's No. 1 crime against business, surpassing employee pilferage, insurance fraud, and embezzlement combined. Robert Half, president of the firm bearing his name, said that time is the most valuable resource to business because it "cannot be replaced, recovered, or replenished".

He defined time theft as leaving work early or arriving late, extended lunch hours, excessive personal phone calls, conducting personal business during company hours, unwarranted sick days, and non-stop chit-chat at the proverbial water cooler.

The study showed the average weekly time theft figure per employee amounted to 4 hours and 22 minutes.

November 14, 1984, San Francisco Chronicle.[66]

---

[66] Quoted in *Philosophy in the Flesh*, by George Lakoff and Mark Johnson, 1999, page 165. Basic Books.

In case you have doubts, and most of us do, about how you think about time I will end this chapter with a process that helps us become aware of our unconscious metaphors of time. The process is designed to take us through a journey from body to mind. It is a way of gaining grounded understanding of how, as Mark Johnson[67] suggests, the body is literally *in* the mind.

Know Your body

Experiential awareness of your body is key to understanding how you think about time. It determines your ability to ground theory into experience. This awareness is, more often than not, subsidiary in nature. That is to say, it guides behaviour and it does so below consciousness. In learning to explore time from the perspective of embodied cognition, our attention needs to be guided to perceive our body as the origin of order in our mind. The visualisation below[68] is designed to achieve this shift of attention. You may choose to create an audio file for the steps, to enable you to listen to the instructions several times as it takes a while to learn to focus your attention this way.

1. Find a comfortable position, either sitting or lying down and you may choose to close your eyes.
2. Consider for a moment what it is like to be your body in space. The many orientational feats you perform as you go through your daily activities. The many *in-out* orientations that may occur in the first few minutes of an ordinary day.
3. You wake up, *out* of sleep and peer *out* from the covers *into* your room, you come *out* of your sleepy state and pull yourself *out of* the bed, climb *into* your dressing gown, have a good stretch, walk *in* a daze *out of* your room and *into* the bathroom, you look *in* the mirror and see your face staring *out at you*....
4. Now turn your attention to your body. Notice that there is a clear boundary between what you perceive as being *in* your

---

[67] *The Body in the Mind*. Mark Johnson, 1987. The University of Chicago Press.
[68] Adapted from Johnson, 1987. A version of the methods that follow were published in an article titled 'Understanding understanding with structuring metaphors (part 2)' by Mariana Funes. *Rapport 39*, Spring 1998.

3. Lived time 103

body and *outside of* it. Trace that boundary *around* your body. Your body is *in* the room and the room *contains* other bodies.
5. Open your eyes. Look around you. Now fix your eyes on one point in the room. Notice that some things are *in* your visual field and others are only *just out of* it. What is in the *centre* of your visual field you can see clearly, and what is on the *periphery* is not so clear, it is fuzzy.
6. Now start gently moving your body and notice that it has many *parts*, your feet, your hands, your arms, and so on.... many parts that form the *whole* of you. What is that like? *Part of a whole*?

Your body in space contains many relationships that organise your experience generally, and your experience of time in particular. Each day you reinforce the reality of these relationships by moving your body in the world in a particular way. You understand *in* and *out*, *part of whole*, *periphery and centre*. It is almost intuitive to understand the world through these relationships. The role our bodies have in our understanding of the world is often forgotten, because in using our ability to abstract we often 'abstract ourselves out of the picture', as Fritjof Capra wisely reminds us.[69] A consequence of this is that we create the illusion of mind and body as separate entities.

Your time metpahor: Understanding time through your body

Metaphorical understanding means that we can understand abstract concepts, in this case time, in terms of the concrete, in this case our body in the world. The metaphor here has the form '**A** is **B**' – the **A**bstract is the **B**ody. We explored examples of this in our exploration of time earlier in this chapter. I suggest you work through this process with somebody else, as it will be easier for him or her to help you notice how you use language. Find a comfortable place for both of you to sit and talk undisturbed. Do the following:

1. Choose a recent event that is related to time in your life (for example, a particularly busy period, your first day on holidays, your strategy to manage 'you' time) and start talking about it.

---

[69] From *The Tao of Physics* by Fritjof Capra, 1975. Shambhala Publications.

2. Your colleague or friend has the task to act *as if* everything s/he hears is true. To do this your partner will, quietly in their mind, cycle through two linked questions as they listen:
   - What could this be true of?
   - Given that it is true, what else has to be true to explain it?

3. Your partner will focus on the A part of the metaphor – as they listen they will be thinking: 'Time is...'and continue to listen to you.

4. Your partner will write down any characteristics of Time that seem to define Time as you talk.
   What you say may, for example, contain the words: *precious nuggets, resource, short supply, can't keep up, saving*

5. Your partner will ask, quietly in their mind, as they continue to listen to you: 'What else in my concrete embodied experience has the characteristics listed in 4 and could structure time?
   This will generate the B-side of the metaphor: *'Time is gold'*, this is a more specific version of 'Time is a limited resource' metaphor.

6. Your partner will then select different characteristics of B that s/he thinks might apply to Time, and ask questions to check that s/he has the appropriate mapping. Continue testing and reflecting back language use until you get an 'Aha moment'. You will suddenly become aware of an image that structures your concept of time.
   For example: *'So how could you get more?'* The question makes sense from within the metaphor: *'I only have a limited amount of gold (time) available'*

7. Once you know one of your time metaphors, help your partner get to one of theirs – the elicitation is also valuable as a tool to increase awareness of the many ways in which the body is the mind.

It is possible to do this process on you own. You can start asking yourself: 'What is my relationship to time?' and write down all that comes to mind as an answer. Once you start writing you do not lift your pen from the paper. Then you can run through the process above using your writing as the starting point for your analysis. However, I suggest you do it with somebody else because it may make it easier to test the accuracy of the elicited metaphor.

If time is understood in terms of metaphors, which are often unique to an individual, then to understand Time we need to know how to elicit each other's metaphors. The value we add to our communication when we choose to refine this skill goes well beyond just building rapport with other people. It allows us to explore the structure of knowledge as a stream of shared meaning where the common currency is our embodied experience. In other words, it is a tool for re-connecting with our body and lived time. We may learn that our metaphor of time is driven by a culture where time is money. Once we know that, we can choose to learn a new vocabulary where time could become a stationary landscape through which we move. So we can stop saying we are out of time, and can start saying that our paths did not take us to that meeting. As we change our words, we change ourselves.

Lived time makes sense, and we feel a need to redefine our sense of time away from the clock. As a generation of choosers we can learn to choose our temporal lifestyles well. We will gain some things, but will have to let go of others. We will not have a healthy sense of time if we continue to be in pursuit of everything.

> *'Late one night we find ourselves going over our net worth in black ink again and again to make sure it is real, still there and still earning the same interest. We need the reassurance that we can define a success at least somewhere in our lives; but the repeated lines of scribbled figures on the legal pad are a sure diagnostic feature that our identity is merging more and more with our bank account. If the nest egg were to disappear, we fret we might disappear too.'*
> David Whyte[70]

---

[70] In *The Heart Aroused: Poetry and the preservation of soul at work*, 1997. The Industrial Society. Thanks to Paul Darling for directing my attention to this great passage.

Lived Time

People who look for a way to continue to go over their net worth each night AND find peace of mind surround me in my work. I hope this book will help them accept the self-evident experiential truth that life shouts out loud and clear, if only we listened – we can live in time or out of time, but we have to choose. If we choose to live in time we may find existential coherence, and through it happiness or Eudemonia, a Greek word meaning a deep sense of well being independent of external events, which stems from a sense of satisfaction with just being alive. We may get peace of mind. Not out in the future, not when we retire but now in the present. As one of my interviewees put it:

'Since I started to work 3 days a week, I just feel so well and rested. It is so nice to be able to wake up to my own time, to be able to get ready at my own pace and then start to work from home. I can follow my own rhythms and that has made such a difference. There are things I cannot do, and yet I don't care because I feel so well and healthy. I had started to believe that I needed all the money that I was earning, when in truth if you just adjust your consumption a little you can live on less. I go to work and feel like I can enjoy it, I can dedicate proper time to the projects I do, rather than feel disconnected from everything because I have to rush to get it all done'.

She has found existential coherence. There is a way to access lived time without giving up the work you do, and without giving up your network of connections at work and outside. This is true if you are willing to make genuine choices. This interviewee can no longer afford to eat out with friends all the time, so she invites them to eat at her home. She now has time to cook.

MAKING THE MOST OF TIME

> *'In the sixties in New Mexico, I used to go to sweat lodges. I would insist on sitting by the door, because if I was anywhere but by the door, I couldn't get out. It would get hotter and hotter and hotter in there, and the steam would fill the space, and I was sure I was going to die. But if I could sit by the door and know that I could leave, then I could make it through. Of course, if I sat away from the door, I had to make it through, but I would be so freaked out the whole time that it wasn't much fun. Well, with true commitment we do not get to sit by the door.'*
> Pema Chodron[71]

Making the most of time is about making a commitment to develop choice on the ways we relate to time. It is about learning to be multi-temporal, and asking questions about the kind of time that is most appropriate for a given purpose. It is about using time as spiritual practice, to learn about ourselves and to ground ourselves in the web of life. We will still have to use clock time for certain purposes, because if we did not we would have to choose 'alternative' lifestyles away from the mainstream. However, we can only make the most of time if we learn that there is life beyond time management, and the conceptualisation of time as money. I have argued that lived time is a healthier conceptualisation, and that it is a positive alternative to clock time. Lived time keeps a connected thread between our past, present and future rather than the disconnected and reductionistic approach to time the clock gives us. The benefits of lived time are an end to our questing for work-life balance, but I want to look at the cost too.

There really aren't enough hours in the day

When we live in clock time we are constantly ignoring our perceptual reality. We say there aren't enough hours in the day, and yet keep

---

[71] In *When Things Fall Apart*, 1997. Shambala Publications.

4. Making the most of time

behaving as if what the statement really meant was the opposite of what it said. It is a crazy way to live, and one that lacks compassion for others and ourselves. Time management makes us ignore our lived experience, and keeps us looking for what we are doing wrong that stops us from finding enough hours in the day. There really are only 168 hours in a week, and not enough hours in the day to keep doing more.

If we choose lived time, we have to start to act on what we say. So, if there aren't enough hours, we stop doing anything that compromises the quality of the means whereby we can achieve a given end. This is a very high price to pay for peace of mind in a clock time world. If I only do that which I can complete with high quality attention, I can no longer do things I now take for granted – keep typing as somebody talks to me on the phone, or read an email as a colleague talks to me in my office, or scan a book for bullet points to get the gist of it quickly.

In other words, I stop adapting to my environment, and start to say enough is enough. I will choose not to do as much, and it is not about my lack of ability. Sigmund Freud talks about two aspects of personal change – he asks if we should adapt to the environment, or if the environment should adapt to us. Our self-improvement ethos rests on the basic assumption that we can and should adapt to our environment. The impact of this approach on our daily life may have become negative, so perhaps we should look at the limitations of assuming that human beings can be, or should be, infinitely adaptable to their environment. This assumption serves political and economic functions. It keeps us working at a frantic pace because if there aren't enough hours in the day it must be because we are not efficient enough, or because we have not developed the right competencies yet. There are those who push back, the 'dot-com' entrepreneurs, self-employed professionals, senior executives who downshift, employees who choose time over money. Often these people have scarce knowledge resources and therefore high bargaining power. They don't have to adapt to the world because they have something the world wants.

For the rest of us, the deeply felt sense of not having enough time to do all that 'needs' to be done, maybe a symptom that we are at the end of the usefulness of clock time living. This is an approach to life that requires us to change faster and faster to stay effective. It is also possible that we really are doing too much, that there really aren't enough hours in the day, and that there is nothing else we need to learn to help us adapt to the pace of life other than doing less and learning to live with the consequences of that. The costs of living exponentially on clock time are high too; we just have to choose what we want to buy.

If we buy lived time, there are consequences to our daily schedule. Imagine that you are going into work and you are going to have a day in lived time. You wake up when you have had enough sleep and get dressed, attending to how it feels to put the clothes on, the feel of the water when you shower. You decide to walk to the station because it is such a nice day. On the way to the station you call Amy, your PA, to let her know that you are on the way, and to check what needs doing when you get in. She tells you that the meeting between the accountants and your Chief Executive started 2 hours ago, and that she sent apologies from you. You get on the train and read a newspaper, and by the time you get into the office you are rested, up to date on the day's news and ready to work. You meet the receptionist as you go in. You take time to chat to her and find out if her house purchase has gone through. You are glad that you took advantage of that flexible time policy as it means you never have to rush into work these days. Only one meeting to attend this morning, you remember the days when you would wake up at 5 to squeeze a third meeting into your morning schedule. You choose not to do that anymore.

Your meeting goes on longer than you expected because you had to stay behind to talk to Tom about his up-coming assessment centre because he was feeling anxious about it. You have lunch with a friend who works in an office nearby during which the phone rings, and Amy tells you that your Chief Executive wants to see you as soon as possible. You say you will be there as soon as possible. But first you finish lunch, catch up with your friend and then you walk back to the office.

You go to see Mary, the Chief Executive, and she wants to know what took you so long. You explain that your health and wellbeing are dependent on you eating and having a break at midday, hence you were doing something important. You explain that you could not work well if you are starved and tired. You have your meeting, which lasts for most of the afternoon. You sit down to finish off some paper work and then head back home. It is 6.00 p.m.

My questions to you to help you reflect on the cost of lived time:

- Would you employ yourself?
- Would you look forward to going into work if your days were like this?
- Would you have the courage to say what needs to be said to protect your time?
- Could you keep your current job if this was the level of activity you allowed yourself?

To create a workplace that supports lived time as a genuine choice will not be easy. To change the beliefs of people at work so you could answer yes to all the above questions is a tall order. However, change starts with the individual choice to develop a healthy sense of time. Employers can help. Joanne Ciulla says: 'If employers want to fill this need for something more, then the answer is not in a prayer meeting or a seminar on finding your soul.'[72] She says that employers should think again about how their workplace is structured, and offer their employees extra time and flexibility so that they can lead healthy lives when not working without fear of being passed over for promotions, bonuses and new jobs.

The problem of the current workplace is that management: 'shun responsibility and maintain power over employees without accountability to them.'[73] However, Ciulla says that employees are held accountable for their own mistakes, but also made accountable for the so-called bad luck – or perhaps mismanagement – of the organization or the economy. Although they may feel empowered, they lack power over their own employment.

When we choose lived time, we take risks. Organisations want employees to be loyal, and work hard, but they can't promise loyalty

---

[72] Page 224 in *The Working Life: The promise and betrayal of modern work*, 2000. Three Rivers Press.
[73] Ibid. Page 230.

in return. When we know this, it is hard to make the choice of lived time. Perhaps it is more honest to admit how hard the choice is than to blame time and work pressures for our unwillingness to take risks. It is hard to take risks with our mortgages and our kid's education, and the risks are real not imagined, if we assume that levels of consumption must stay the same. If we are not willing to pay the price of lived time, perhaps the best we can do is learn to be compassionate towards our fears, rather than blaming ourselves or others for not making certain lifestyle changes.

Developing a healthy sense of time

If you are ready to develop a healthier sense of time that includes lived time, then you need to take the long view on learning, like the Dalai Lama[74]. This is not something that can be 'accelerated', and may well take many lifetimes! The Dalai Lama proposes a set of stages that are needed for an individual to learn a new way of being,

1. We must educate ourselves – what are the consequences and implications of living in clock time? What are the negative consequences of keeping things the same? Urgency for change only comes with a comprehensive examination of how the way I live today is stopping my ability to be happy
2. Over time we develop conviction – we become more committed to a practice as we develop a sense of conviction through education that our current lifestyle is hindering us.
3. We become determined – the conviction that change is needed leads to the determination to change
4. We start to act – only now are we ready to start doing what needs to be done to change
5. We become willing to keep making the effort – the strong determination to change enables one to make a sustained effort to establish new habits, the habit of lived time for example.

---

[74] From *The Art of Happiness* by His Holiness The Dalai Lama and H. Cutler, 1998. Riverhead Books.

4. Making the most of time

The Dalai Lama tells us: 'This is the way that inner change and transformation take place in all things, no matter what you are trying to accomplish' The path to change for him is Buddhist practice. In Buddhist practice we develop a sense of urgency through reflection on the impermanence of human life, confidence and enthusiasm are found through reflection on the preciousness of human experience, and the experiential understanding of both of these leads us to want to use every precious moment of life to learn. 'By making steady effort we can overcome any form of negative conditioning and make positive changes in our lives. But you still must realise genuine change does not happen overnight'.

The Dalai Lama uses his own development as an example: 'Now for example, in my own case, I think if I compare my normal state of mind today to, say, twenty or thirty years ago, there is a big difference.' He points out that the difference he reached came step by step. 'I started to learn Buddhism at the age of 5 or 6, but at that time I had no interest in Buddhist teachings although I was called the highest re-incarnation.' The Dalai Lama continues that he thinks it was not until he reached about 16 years old that he began to develop serious feelings about Buddhism, and tried to begin serious practice. Over many years he started to develop a deep appreciation of Buddhist principles and practices. At the beginning, practices that seemed impossible and almost unnatural for him became increasingly natural and easy to relate to. 'This occurred through gradual familiarisation. Of course, this process took more than forty years.' The Dalai Lama's Buddhist practice is with him all his life; he practises as an end in itself, not to achieve an end point.

If we compare his time frames for change and learning with those of the 'hare-brained executive' that has to get it right first time, or with that of the 'accelerated learning' approach to learning, that promises change in half the time, we see clock time addiction at work. We feel a sense of entitlement to do it and to do it quickly. We feel discouraged when development happens at a slow rate. The Dalai Lama suggests we deal with our slowness not with impatience, but with meditation and compassion. He suggests that we take a long-term view, and stand back when encountering obstacles. There are things in life that take time to take root and cannot be accelerated.

One of those things is our ability to change our habits of body, speech and mind. However, we do need a discipline that allows us to refine our perception enough that we can really see those habits. Our skill in self-deception makes this hard to accomplish.

Developing a healthy time sense requires compassion, patience and discipline. It requires a long-term view of learning, and questions the wisdom of asking of ourselves and of those around us that we become effective learners, by which we often just mean 'do it faster'. Certain human processes take time, and to try to rush or accelerate them may seem as foolish as the old saying: 'sleep fast, we need the pillows'.

Obstacles in life are an integral part of life and a way in to develop a sense of time that makes sense. And doing this is not an easy task, as Jonson[75] tells us: 'Time is not something you can resolve once and for all. You're probably going to have to do as I do: keep at it all your life...' Jonson uses the analogy of going up and down a staircase with four steps. 'To take the first step you have to start getting used to thoughts about time other than such depressing statements as "I just don't have enough time!" "There's no time!"' You can just stand there and ask yourself: 'I don't know how I'm going to find the time.' Or, standing on the first step, you can begin to realise you actually have other ways of relating to time beyond narrowing it down. When you reach the second step it means you have discovered some better methodical ways of reflecting on your time and how you use it. If you manage to reach the third step, you will have learned to describe your thoughts about time, and how you live life to the full in the middle of ongoing time. Jonson concludes: 'On the fourth step you can pause for a bit and imagine that you've understood everything that's important for your relationship to time.' So, we need patience, discipline and a practice. We need to learn to work with time and get comfortable going up and down those 4 steps of time awareness.

Meditations in time

In talking about the Dalai Lama and his long-term view of developing new habits I am not suggesting you become a Buddhist monk to

---

[75] In *Unwinding the Clock* by Bodil Jonson, 2001. Harcourt.

develop a healthy sense of time, although it would certainly achieve that result. However, I am suggesting that you need to establish a 'Lived Time practice'. Most religions use some form of meditation or contemplation as spiritual practice. The aim of a practice is just that, to practice. Meditation allows us to stop doing what we normally do and learn to pay attention to our mind and body. If we use meditation in lived time practice we can learn to notice the habits of mind and body that clock time is encouraging in us. The point is to have a discipline that teaches to stop and notice, and that teaches us to refine our attention. To develop a healthy sense of time we need some form of attention training – we have to pay attention to attention.

My discipline over the years has been The Alexander Technique. It started as a 'quick fix' for backache rather than a meditation in time, but it is now my main tool for learning lived time. I believe that meditation is a tool that needs to become part and parcel of our day if it is to teach us about lived time. The Technique has worked for me precisely because its practice is embedded in day-to-day living. The technique has been my teacher for 13 years, and through it I have recovered from crippling back pain that doctors could only cure with anaesthetic injections. Why deal with the cause if you can tackle the symptom? The back pain, however, went away after the first few months of Alexander Technique after I learned enough about it to keep the pain at bay. I also started to glimpse a more important change. I would catch myself at moments in time just before my mind started racing, just before I started rushing around to get to my end goal that bit quicker, just before I lost sight of my body because some interesting thought caught my attention. The sense of urgency to practice came from my need to keep the pain away, and in practising I began to catch my habits of mind and body.

It was only a glimpse initially and then I would just get caught into the whirlwind of my hectic life. Then it would be time for another lesson in the technique with my teacher. Lessons are generally one to one and not in groups. My teacher would ask me to stay quiet inside and out as we worked with the technique. We would sit, stand, walk, and do other everyday activities. The way they were done in the lesson always felt different from my everyday behaviour. I used to find him, and the lessons, boring. He did not want to analyse and talk about all the changes that started to happen in my body and mind as I followed the simple instructions the technique teaches. But I would stop mentally and physically and again get a glimpse of what it was like to be at peace with my body and my mind.

As soon as the lesson was over, my mind would start to race again. I had so much to do, so many people to phone, and so many items to cross off my must-do-list. In the end, what I wanted to achieve always became more important than the means whereby I would work towards a goal. I was compelled to set a goal and go for it, irrespective of the personal cost of getting it done. Achieving the goal was the sole purpose of my life. It did not matter that my back would hurt, or that as I lost myself in my end-gaining I also lost the ability to be present with myself. I kept booking my lessons, I kept finding them boring, and I kept practising. I could feel deep down that here was a discipline with the potential to teach me to live my life in a different way, a way that could give me peace of mind. However, there was discomfort each time I had a lesson in learning that I could not choose. I could not choose how to move my body without tensing unnecessary muscles, and I could not choose to keep my mind quiet to give myself the instructions of the technique. My need to analyse and talk could only be controlled for short periods of time. I would not stay present with myself for long, as I would start to think of the past – what was it that just happened on the way to the station? Or I would start to think of the future – I think I will go to visit mum after the lesson.

I continue to practice today without any extraordinary aim in mind. My only aim is to 'become profoundly ordinary', as Lewis Richmond suggests, and just learn to turn up to my moment-to-moment experience. Each moment contains within it infinite choice, and the technique teaches me that there is a way to be which gives you real choice each moment. You can learn to be: 'always on your way to somewhere, never quite settling on any fixed place', consciously deciding what to attend to next without being driven by a clock or by a deadline. This is my practice, to develop my ability to attend and notice my habits of mind and body that contribute to my clock time life.

Without the sustained effort of a practice the learning disappears. This is not just a task to get done; it is a task to keep doing. The rest of this chapter offers you other profoundly ordinary practices for you to commit to doing if you choose for the rest of your life. If you have an interest in developing a formal practice such as the Alexander Technique[76], then contact the Association for Teachers of the Alexander Technique in England. If you want to pursue Buddhist meditation practices there are many books[77] and internet resources freely given to help you find a method that works for you. Simple instructions for formal meditation practice can be found in Pema Chodron's book *When things fall Apart*, referred to earlier in the book. I have also included an appendix written by the Reverend Andrew Hunter with simple non-denominational meditation instructions.

The rest of this chapter is about day-to-day practices to develop our ability to be in lived time. Firstly, we pay attention to attention, then talk about the value of inefficiency. We will also look at the value of repetition and routine. The practices are about ways of developing a connection with our past and our future in a living present. For example, our sense of the future would be very different if we expanded our mind to think of a future 200 years from now, and made our daily actions and our goals for the future consistent with this notion.

A living Present: On the art and science of attention[78]

A sense of a present that is alive requires us to develop what Buddhists call a serviceable mind. If we are unable to attend to anything for more than 3 seconds without distraction, as has been demonstrated by modern neuroscience, it is hardly surprising that we are not able to attend to our present when we choose to, our past when we need guidance, or our future when we need inspiration.

---

[76] A simple introduction can be found in *Alexander Technique* by Chris Stevens, 1987. Optima.
[77] For example, read *Work as Spiritual Practice* by Lewis Richmond, 1999. Is an excellent book on using Buddhist principles in everyday life. It has many daily practices that can be applied by clock time addicts to develop a healthy sense of time, though its aim is spiritual development.
[78] I owe the title to this section to 'Notes from a marine biologist's daughter: On the art and science of attention' by Anne McCrary Sullivan. *Harvard Educational Review*, Vol. 70, no2, summer, 2000.

Attention is our ability to put our sensory awareness onto an object and concentrate on that object as we choose. In reality we are not able to do this for very long without getting distracted. In the complexity of our lives our attention is constantly being diverted to many different things in our environment. We rarely keep any free attention to focus on what is going on inside our bodies. One way to help you gain understanding is to think of your ability to attend as having the shape of an hourglass. From your attention being very diffuse and external you can move to a state of attention that is internal and focused. You can move at will from a state of broad attention to one of concentrated attention. Try this experiment: find one thing in the external world to focus on. It may be a sound or it may be a colour. As you keep your attention on that external focus you can allow yourself to be aware of something going on for you internally. So, as I hear the sound of water, I can notice the temperature in my fingertips. This starts to get your attention focused. One thing outside and one thing inside. The idea is to use your internal dialogue to tell yourself: 'As I... (external focus), I can... (internal focus)'.

Your internal focus can be a feeling, a thought or a memory. As you keep focusing, you will lose the conscious attention on the external object and your attention will expand internally. You will become conscious of your breathing, your thoughts, and other body sensations. You will connect with the world that is going on in your internal experience. Hence, the notion of an hourglass, wide at the top, then narrow in the middle, and finally wide again at the bottom. This process[79] allows you to absorb into your own internal experience and to start to focus. The symbol below appears throughout this chapter to indicate specific activities for you to do.

⧗

Training your attention

Find a quiet place where you will not be disturbed, and sit down. Have a clock that can sound an alarm and can be set to 3-minute intervals.

---

[79] I learnt this process from Brent Geary. He may be contacted at www.erickson-foundation.org .

You will need to set the clock 7 times. Focus on one external sound, which could be the sound of the clock. Set the alarm for your first 3 minutes. Find a spot with your eyes and focus on that spot until the alarm rings. Now set the clock again. Direct your attention to something the mind sees until the alarm rings. Your focus for the rest of the 3-minute slots are: as you hear the clock, focus on one area of your body until the alarm rings; as you hear the clock, focus on a sound of nature you can hear in your mind; as you hear the clock, focus on a pleasant emotion until the alarm rings; as you hear the clock, see yourself over there looking at yourself sitting; as you hear the clock, focus on a memory you treasure. This is a practice. You will get distracted and you will lose your focus. Notice that this happens, and then come back to your object of attention. If you get impatient, tell yourself 'impatience' and come back to your object. The benefit of this practice is that you develop your ability to attend at will, and slowly learn to quieten distractions.

There are no easy answers, but you can shift your behaviour in these small ways each day of your life. You can commit to a practice and develop the discipline needed to learn to use your mind – to have it be silent when you want to, focused on specific images when you want, and generally able to attend to your inner and outer world at will. You cannot develop a healthy sense of time until you have developed your ability to attend. You cannot develop your mind until you can pay attention. You learn to attend to the subtleties of how and who you are right now. Your job is just to notice detail, like an artist might.

In her article on attention Sullivan reflects on ways to educate the attention. She talks about her own life as having been grounded in attention as the daughter of a marine biologist always tagging along with mum to look for 'stuff'. How does it develop? Can we teach attention? And interestingly, given our purposes, she asks if attention to external reality may make it easier to become aware of internal reality and if: 'focused attention to an immediate reality may engage memory and imagination.' She believes that attention enlivens the senses and makes the senses 'wake up to where they are'.

She also talks of the need for aesthetic vision to engage our:

'sensitivity to suggestion, to pattern, to that which is beneath the surface as well as to the surface itself.' This kind of vision requires that we attend to detail and to form: 'the perception of relations; the perception of nuances; and the perception of change'. So to develop a sense of time go to exhibitions, learn to draw, play with clay, make sand castles, or: 'Stare. It is the way to educate your eye, and more. Stare, pry, listen, eavesdrop. Die knowing something. You are not here long.' [80]

Attention can help us develop a better relationship with time, according to Sullivan, one with choice: 'Aesthetic vision adjusts the flow of time. It may seize a moment in order to stare at it more fully, more deeply'. It can seize and perceive its flux and its potential for change. We need to be embedded in experience in order to attend. We develop what James Hillman calls precision consciousness this way. The clock removes us from our experience, and hence our ability to attend to the world and each other is diminished. She believes that our perception of the present moment can contain the past and the present: 'Aesthetic vision does not assume that what one sees in the moment is what one always will see.' She says that aesthetic vision perceives the potential for transformation: 'within any apparent fixity – a block of wood, a piece of clay, a display of words, the configuration of a classroom or the behaviour of an individual child' it is possible for us to use aesthetic vision to connect to our sense of time. Like an artist seeing the potential of a block of wood, we can seize each moment and see the potential in it, see what is in the surface and what is beneath the surface.

Efficiency does not allow us to stay with a moment for very long. Clock time living requires that we use a given moment for more and more activities. What we gain in 'efficiency', we lose in the quality of interaction with each moment. This is a reason why we can use aesthetic vision to develop a different kind of relationship with each moment beyond what the efficiency of clock time allows. As we keep expanding the number of events we put in that given point in time our lives become starved of depth. Our attention can only cover the surface level of, say, ten events at a given time, we cannot explore all

---

[80] By Walker Evans, quoted in Sullivan, 2000.

that a given moment can contain. We cannot treat all we encounter as if it were alive and give it the attention it deserves. To belong to an Anima Mundi is to swap efficiency for service to the world. Aesthetic vision can be an entry point to this way of living.

If we develop the quality of attention contained in aesthetic vision in our everyday life at work, and outside of work, the transformation can be substantial. Everyday life can feed our soul, just as poetry does: 'when we listen to poetry we can experience a sense of relief. Thank god somebody else feels that!' says David Whyte. He tells us that a quality of deep attention is required to access our imagination, although we find this depth of attention frightening. This is because it requires us to come face to face with our dark side, the aspects of ourselves we have neglected, the aspects of ourselves that make us less than perfect and more imperfectly human. Deep attention can help us let go of our self-deceptions, and develop a sense of lived time. Deep attention forces us to let go of quantity.

⌛

Anne McCrary Sullivan's attention practice 1

'I was always searching for ways to bring students into attention, the sort of deep attention that would elicit the capacity for poetry that I believed they all had in them...take them out on the broad lawn, spread out, each to sit alone and watch a small patch of grass, to observe and record "what happens there".' Do this next time you sit in the park. Stay with your patch of grass long enough to get to know it.

⌛

Anne McCrary Sullivan's attention practice 2

'In another homework assignment, I would ask them to 'find a place where there is nothing going on. Sit there for ten minutes and record everything that happens'. The important thing is that you stay with your practice for the 10 minutes and keep staring.

Our perception needs a lot of sharpening up. The lenses of attention need polishing, and in order to enter a time that makes sense we must stare well.

Silence

> *A day of silence*
> *Can be a pilgrimage in itself.*
>
> *A day of silence*
> *Can help you listen*
> *To the soul play*
> *Its marvellous lute and drum*
>
> *Is not most talking*
> *A crazed defence of a crumbling fort?*
> Hafiz[81]

This poem is an example of attending to the depth of the moment. As I read this poem I am reminded of a conversation long ago when a friend mentioned Hafiz to me. Last year at a course I run at my business school I talked about a poem I could not find. A week later, a book came through the post. It is a wonderful gift to be heard; one of the participants on the course had tracked down the title of the book that contained my poem, and had bought and sent me the book as a way of saying thank you. Today, as I pick up the book (the surface) to look for a poem that talks about silence, I have a choice. I can scan the poem with no attention, 2 minutes and a moment without meaning. Or I can take time to hold the book, remember its history, think of the people who participated in its history and take the time to type the words savouring their wisdom, 20 minutes of clock time, and a moment of lived time that feeds my soul. An experience of deep attention from which I feel nourished and satisfied. I want to live as

---

[81] In *I Heard God laughing – Renderings of Hafiz* by Daniel Ladinsky, 1996. Mobius Press.

many days of my life as I can like this. Attending to attention helps me to have more days like this each year. Or put more simply by the Japanese:

> *More fragrant*
> *Because of the one*
> *Who saw and picked them*
> *These flowers*
> *Precious, transient*
> Isumi Shikibu[82]

Maya Angelou Days and other stopping activities

Wake up early and get ready for your day. Dressed and fed. Walk out of that door without any idea of what you will do for the day. Maya Angelou has days like this once a month. Or you can take all day to cook dinner for close friends and family. Or spend a morning cleaning a silver tray, or any treasured family heirloom. Or you can go for a drive that takes you nowhere, think of the trees coming towards you rather than you heading towards the trees, and feel still in movement.

Developing our deep attention requires what Pema Chodron calls right effort. She defines the right kind of effort as the sort of effort that we make when we are camping up in the mountains. We wake up on a cold morning, and the warmth of the sleeping bag calls us to stay inside, but as we think of the lovely walk that we have to look forward to on this crisp sunny day, we make the effort to get up and make our breakfast. We have to make right effort to keep turning up to the practice of deep attention.

A living present – the art of slow reading

Another practice to develop our ability to perceive the past and the future in the moment is one that comes from the Catholic religion.

---

[82] In *The Ink Dark Moon* by Isumi Shikibu, 1986. Vintage Classics.

Benedictine monks, amongst others, practice what is called 'lectio divina'. It means divine reading. When I first came across the practice, I was given a piece of paper as I sat down in the chapel. I was lost staring at a bit of the bible that made little sense to me, as I was unaccustomed to reading sacred texts. I was also given written instructions on the process:

1. We find a quiet place and a quiet mind to allow us to direct our attention to the text
2. We ask that we be helped to understand, and for life to remove from our mind and heart all that makes us unreceptive to understanding this text. We find a sense of giving ourselves over to our reading
3. We ask our ancestors to accompany us in our reading
4. We read a little, slowly forming the words with our lips, keeping our hearts alert, letting the words find their way to our heart, we keep our mind attentive
5. When something strikes us, we stop. We repeat the phrase several times. Let it sink into our heart
6. Our response – how does this word affect us? Is it a word of correction or encouragement?
7. We stay with the word until we have received all the nourishment that is possible from it
8. We keep reading for the time we have allowed
9. We end by making some resolution as a result of what we have read
10. We write down anything that strikes us while we read

This is an active process, but one that does not put the individual and her intellect in the driving seat. We attend and allow ourselves to be guided by the words and our emotional responses to the words. We have to keep repeating what strikes us, so that we can understand beyond the surface level and allow associations to come to consciousness. We have to be mindful of our past, and ask our ancestors to walk with us in the present to help our understanding. We then become aware that we are reading a story that has been read repeatedly over centuries and in many languages. We start to feel the 'ground' of our present, our past. And then, as we in this present moment become a link to the future, we are asked to make a resolution for the future.

I wish that I could teach slow-reading instead of speed-reading in my management courses. I believe our relationship to time and life would change if we did more slow reading in our lives. Just 30 minutes of this kind of reading can put us in touch with the depth of the moment. My initial speed-read took only 5 minutes but I had no connection with the words beyond the surface level of the words. This is our dilemma; we have been trading quality for quantity for so long that we no longer see that there is another way. Or if we do, we see that we would 'lose' out materially if we follow it.

I apply this 'slow reading method' to many things in my life. I discovered the first time that my '5 minute speed read' led me to a quick judgement that dismissed the words in front of me, and I wanted to move on to the next interesting thing. The '30-minute slow read', was a shared experience with a group, with my past, with my future, and it gave me a sense of my place in the world, irrespective of whether or not I used the construct of God to explain my experience. Slow reading helps us connect with our imagination, gives us a way to understand ourselves, and helps us connect to a sense of place.

And why not slow decision making too?
This really challenges the received view of clock time. We like to believe that quick decisions are good decisions. Lived time asks us to make good decisions that are based on quality not quantity. Quick decisions may sometimes be good decisions, but not always. To work on your decision-making in lived time, I suggest a practice created by Lewis Richmond, which he calls working with a question[83].

You first ask yourself 'What is my question?' You might want to start with a question as simple as: 'What should I do?' The second stage is to repeat the question to yourself as you go through your day, and as you pay deep attention to what is going on around you. You are not trying to rationally answer the question, you are just holding the question in your mind as, for example, you walk. If the question

---

[83] From *Work as Spiritual Practice* by Lewis Richmond, 1999. Page 47.

seems to evolve or change as you hold the question, let it do so. The third stage is to follow the question where it leads; to a new question, or to one word that now represents the question in your mind. You let the question 'move under, around, and through your life, looking for a way through.'[84] The final stage is to settle the question. You do this in a number of ways: you find the answer, you establish a new question, or you just forget the question. All are valid ways of settling the question. This process allows your unconscious mind to work on the decision making process. Your conscious mind wants a quick decision to move on to the next thing quickly. You unconscious mind can bring in other criteria to the decision, such as lived time and your wellbeing. So, you raise the question, you repeat the question, you follow the question and you settle the question.

A living present: Shield the inefficiencies that remain

We must 'shield the inefficiencies that remain', proclaimed a newspaper headline I read long ago. We find lived time in what clock time labels inefficient. Once I took time to have lunch with my bank manager, and that was inefficient. I still remember the joy I had driving to the city in my first flash car, to show my bank manager what his money had bought. Childish and unnecessary, shrieks clock time.

> *Only in silence the word,*
> *Only in dark the light,*
> *Only in dying life:*
> *Bright the hawk's flight*
> *On an empty sky*
> Ursula Le Guin[85]

That which feeds our imagination and gives us a sense of wellbeing is in what David Abram calls the modes of invisibility. These are the spider webs that are not visible but are touchable, and the associations that come when I stay with something beyond my initial judgement. The air we breathe, a mode of invisibility we are dependent on and yet is

---

[84] Ibid. page 49
[85] In *The Earthsea Quartet* by Ursula Le Guin, 1993. Penguin Books.

4. Making the most of time

mostly absent from our conscious awareness. Not all that counts can be counted. Abram calls air: 'The soul of the visible landscape, the secret realm from whence all beings draw their nourishment'. The ecological dangers of ignoring that which is immediately absent from awareness are obvious.

From a temporal perspective, the assumption that the surface and the seen are all that is real has led us to a relationship with time that is starving the very essence of who we are. Preserving the inefficiencies that remain and even creating a little more inefficiency in our lives might give us a better quality of life. We look for efficiency in our relationships too, and our relationships suffer. If we do not find a balance between getting things done superficially in less time, and doing them in-depth but taking more time, the possibility of genuine relationship at work and outside is diminished. Look for what exists in the absences. Dare to be inefficient.

> *'How do you handle the notes as well as you do?'*
>
> *The pianist answered:*
> *'I handle the notes no better than many others, but the pauses – ahh!*
> *That is where the art resides.'*
> Arthur Rubinstein[86]

Instead of sending that email, what if you decided to arrange a lunch with your work colleague to talk about what would have taken you 2 minutes to write? The idea of 'having more than we need' to achieve a given result is present in many contexts. It is called redundancy. We need it in language to be able to express ourselves, and we need it in bits of information in computers in order to preserve accuracy, as we need it to function. If we applied the principle of 'doing more with less' to our bits of information, those emails you send so fast would never reach the recipient making the same sense that you intended. The data would corrupt on the way.

---

[86] Quoted in *Timeshifting* by Stephan Rechtschaffen, 1996. Rider Books.

An example of redundancy in language is gossip. And perhaps gossip is as important as those redundant bits of data in our emails. It is not efficient, but it is important. It is not purposeful, but it is important. It is a way of making a web-work, a way of connecting to others at work. In these days of no extended family, and no sense of place, we buy our gossip from a magazine. These sell well, telling us about the lives of strangers. This fulfils a human expectation of belonging and connection that is not being met in other ways. Clock time moves us more and more towards efficient, I-It modes of relating and working. An inefficient I-Thou mode may not get as many superficial things done, but will preserve the depth of relationship we simultaneously destroy and crave for.

⌛

Catch yourself wanting to be efficient and stop it

You will hear yourself wanting to terminate a conversation because 'it is not going anywhere'. You will think of calling a friend you have not spoken to for a while, and decide you can't 'because you have too much to do'. 4 times a day when you catch yourself wanting to be efficient in this way – just stop it – allow yourself to be splendidly inefficient!

We think of efficiency as sufficient reason to act in the world. If giving doctors a 2-minute target per patient means they see more patients, then they are more efficient. The action is justified just by the bottom line of efficiency. When I talk about shielding the inefficiencies that remain, I mean that our actions should be determined by more than just how efficient any one action is. To help us with this we might go back to the Aristotelian notion of efficient cause. The fact that I can cause something to happen, efficiently or otherwise, is a necessary but not a sufficient reason for me to do that thing. Aristotle sees efficient cause as only one of 4 possible causes for action.

I have come across this notion as explained by James Hillman[87] and have found it a profound way of choosing my actions according

---

[87] In *Kinds of Power*. 1995. Currency Doubleday.

4. Making the most of time

to a life beyond clock time. Aristotle's answer to the question why was divided up into 4 causes. We act because of a formal cause – the idea or essence of an action. We act because of a final cause – the aim or purpose of that action. We act because of a material cause – the effect in the tangible world of our action, what we act on. We act because of an efficient cause – because we can initiate action in the world. All are necessary for correct action in the world. James Hillman believes that efficient cause is not sufficient justification for human action. He says that the efficient cause makes things happen, but: 'When it is singled out as the only cause, then it does not matter what happens, to what or whom it happens and for what purpose it happens.'[88]

We can turn this idea into 4 basic questions to help us decide on correct action:

- Can I do it more efficiently?
- What are the effects of doing it more efficiently? How am I affecting the material world?
- What is the essence, the principle, behind this action?
- What is that for the sake of which my action is performed?

I have now reduced these questions to a sentence. I fill in the blanks when I am trying to decide how to act. I do (the action) to (the material I act on), for the sake of (my purpose) and with the intent of (the ethical or aesthetic principle behind the action). I write on my computer for the sake of creating a book, and with the intent of sharing my ideas with others. It is a great practice that has highlighted for me how often in our life the final cause has become the bottom line: 'which provides the philosophical ground for the heightened purism of efficiency at the expense of the other two causes, material and formal'[89]. Clock time assumes that efficiency is the final cause for action. If we can do it, we do it. And if we can do it in less time, that is even better. The 4 questions for correct action may help us start to make the most of our time beyond just being efficient, and always doing more with less.

---

[88] Ibid. Page 38.
[89] Ibid. Page 41

Doctors can see patients in 2 minutes and this is an efficient use of time. However, the effects of doing this are that patients feel used and not listened to. The principle behind the action is to make more money, either for the insurance company, or for the government. It is done for the purpose of getting the most and giving the least. The 4 questions yield the morality (or lack of it) of our actions. Those who give doctors these targets might like to read this paragraph alongside the old dictum 'primum nihil nocere', first do no harm. We stay trapped in clock time, because to make the most of time asks us to come face to face with the inconsistency of our actions.

The past into the present: focus on stability rather than change

Stability deserves attention. Organisational and personal change are the currency of our organisations today. We have departments dedicated to change, masters degrees on how to be a change agent, business schools have consultants specialising in change, and many organisations pay significant amounts of money to consultants to help them manage change, and to help people buy into change initiatives. We know of many initiatives that fail, and many a failed initiative is not reported in management journals. I spend my life in organisations giving people time to reflect on how to cope with the speed of change around them, speed that comes either from planned initiatives, or from the incoherent entanglement of the self-preserving goals of individuals in different departments.

The comment I hear most often is that people can't cope with the speed of change around them. This inability to cope is driving them to attend training courses to develop a set of competencies that sometimes read like a job description for God. What is never challenged is the notion that the speed of change will just keep getting faster, and that the only way to handle this is by accelerating change within ourselves.

However, many brilliant thinkers have questioned and continue to question the wisdom of constantly increasing our speed. Gandhi admonished that there was more to life than increasing its speed. Gunther Siegmund Stent[90] predicted that every progressive cumulative

---

[90] In *The Coming of the Golden Age: A View of the End of Progress*, 1969. Doubleday.

enterprise, such as science, technology, and the arts, would come to an end. These human endeavours, he argued, were likely to be moving at a fast rate just before they come to a halt. Ultimately, as they became less practical, further removed from our experience and more expensive society would decline, and the world would be left in a largely static condition.

We may be running very fast to nowhere. The speed of change will keep getting faster until society comes to a halt as it declines and breaks up in the name of efficiency. But we can stop grooming ourselves for change and start attending to stability. We can attend to the cyclical nature of life, and detach our attention from our expectation of unprecedented events. The myths and stories of oral traditions, for example, create a coherent narrative of past and present by foregrounding that which repeats. Historically, once man starts to note that which is unique and unprecedented we shift our sense of time from the cycles of nature to that of linear clock time. Simon Biggs, professor of social gerontology at Keele University, says: 'Research backs up the importance of continuity throughout life and it has shown that people need to have a convincing narrative story of who they are and where they have been. They need to be grounded. There are so many influences pulling you in different directions nowadays. We need a way to make sense of who we are in the present'.

However, modern work and life require that we praise the god of flexibility. Richard Sennett argues against the value of flexibility. He equates it with the idea of no long term. Teams keep changing, and we tell employees that they must learn to deal with ambiguity and change to succeed. This may be only wishful thinking on the part of our organisations. In truth, flexibility keeps us in a state of fight-flight, and we need continuity to be healthy. Flexibility and a workplace with no long-term outlook encourage surface relationships, a scripted type of conversation based on task and not relationship. Sennett supports the notion of depth instead. What I call deep attention includes some sense of the long-term. It helps us create the coherent narrative we need, and go beyond the surface of what is going on in our relationships.

Sennett sees unstable employment as leading to 'the corrosion of character'. He tells us that the lack of this long-term commitment makes us feel disoriented, destroys trust and makes us behave in ways the organisation values, but disconnects our motivation from this behaviour. We almost become actors on a stage, and in this metaphor, training courses are the drama schools where managers learn the script. He believes that long-term relationships are the only way to avoid the disconnection. Joanne Ciulla believes that there may be other ways, such as respect and truth telling. She argues that you can have short-term bonds where you tell the truth and respect others. This is not evident in our working lives at present. She says that the most common lies told in the workplace are about performance. Employees have an inaccurate view of what they bring to work. Managers often take the easy route as: 'it is easier and less-time consuming to tell people that they are above average than to tell them they are below it and why'. I agree with her analysis that bad performance is often glossed over at work, and I also agree with Sennett in that I see the cause of this as having to do with the short-term nature of our bonds. We do need stability to have a good quality of life and work. In terms of a healthy sense of time, making personal choices that reinforce what is stable is hard to do in today's climate. Still, we find a way through our informal networks, and could more often challenge the assumption that change is always good in our daily conversations.

Mary Catherine Bateson[91] talks about the need to focus on the continuity that exists within change. We sometimes have to change behaviour in order to preserve an important value: 'We have to change in order to preserve what we always meant'. She uses the example of fairness to explain her point. In order to preserve what as a society we always intended by being fair to all, we have had to change our behaviour towards blacks and women. She also talks about the importance of ritual to help give us a sense of continuity. We have changed the content of rituals through time, but it is important to preserve the function of ritual as a way to give us continuity and stability. We can, and should, create new rituals. Change is necessary. What we need to remember, she tells us, is that when we change

---

[91] In 'Continuity, change and Intuition', 1997. NLP Comprehensive Conference.

we are: 'Merely putting together the familiar in unfamiliar ways'. Attending to what is familiar is as important as putting it together in new ways. The familiar preserves core values, the unfamiliar gives us a way of keeping our experience fresh and relevant to our current situation.

Wisdom is not just about having been around a long time, it is about having been around and having accumulated relevant experience. In not valuing the familiar, we are rupturing the thread of the past into our present. Promises and our word become meaningless. So for example, I read in the paper today that a bank that offered high interest 'for life' will cease trading after a few months in existence. It will give compensation to its current customers for the trouble it has caused. The broken promise does not matter, because the customers will get money. The problem will be handled efficiently, but other causes for action will not be explored. When we live in a world where 'for life' can mean 6 months, we need new rituals that help us connect with what is stable in our lives. Our attention is normally trained to focus on time and movement, but we must regain our focus on place and permanence.

Many disciplines teach us to do this. Dancers learn core stability, Buddhists learn equanimity, the Alexander Technique teaches about primary directions for effortless body use. In our need to keep up – Go fast! Upgrade! Be efficient! Do more with less now! – we have lost the perception of what is constant and stable. We see it all changing faster and faster. It is. Mary Catherine Bateson asks her undergraduate classes: 'What have you taught your parents?' After an initial hesitation – you are, after all, supposed to learn from your parents, not teach them – her graduates remember that they had to teach their parents how to program the video machine, how to use the computer, a particular computer game, how to listen to rap music, and how to save the planet by using cloth napkins. Things do change faster and faster and hence wisdom is to 'remain open to learning'. But there are also things in each moment and in our environment, which are constant and that never change. Can you name them? The need for quick perception has made us immune to similarity, so we notice what is different. But we can re-train our perception and this poem below will help us.

I work in the area of creativity and innovation. I see the impact of the focus on change rather than on stability here too. Systemic creativity tells us that true innovation is only possible when we have a sound grasp of what has gone on before us, a domain of expertise, before we can innovate. We learn rules before we can deviate from them. Developing this knowledge takes time, often years. Only then can we apply our creative thinking to contribute something new to this body of knowledge. We need to learn about what is stable before we can change it.

When I am asked to develop people's creativity, it is often understood as an individual pursuit, and one that can be learnt independently of a domain and a field. The focus on change leads to the assumption that any change is good, so creativity is about generating ideas (any idea). When I talk to people on my courses about the aspects of creativity that are about building from the past, the gap in the knowledge of their domain is often huge. Most have not been in their jobs for more than a couple of years, and are being asked to generate ideas for an organisation that may have a 100 years of history.

⌛

Focus on similarity for a day

Go to work and attend to what has remained the same since you joined. Review your past at work, and think about the present. Rather than focus on what should change, ask yourself: What happens now when work is at its best, and what if I did more of what is already working in the future?

The past into the present: Repetition and routine

I was listening to a tape the other night about a particular Buddhist teaching I am learning for my meditation practice. The teacher was telling the story of the teaching through history. The story covered many centuries and many places. It told of the man who had gone all the way from India to Indonesia to find the teachings that had been lost; how he had found them not in written form but in the form of a teacher that passed them on to him. How he had then taken many years to write them down, and had then gone to Nepal and taken the teachings with him. Many years had passed and the teachings had been lost and found again, until in the more recent past, they have been followed and taught to the master from whom this teacher had learnt. She had taken many years to practice and learn them, and had now also written a book on her understanding of the teachings. I was left with such a strong sense of an unbroken lineage all the way back to the days when the teachings had been created. And now I was listening to and learning the same teachings.

Repeating the patterns of the past is how we keep in touch with our past. This is not to say that we don't innovate nor do things differently; we do the familiar in unfamiliar ways. For example, I was now listening to an audio file in my computer, where in the past men had to travel thousands of miles to find the same teachings. We keep the essence of the pattern and thus the continuity through repetition. With meditation it is the same. We are taught the form of meditation, often differently depending on who you learn it from, and follow the same form that has been followed for thousands of years by our ancestors.

Most religious festivals and rituals are focused on remembering events that happened thousands of years ago. As our culture has become less religious we have lost this way of accessing our past through repetition in ritual. We have also become removed from the institutions, such as royalty, that keep us connected with the past, whatever else they do or do not do politically. Sennett suggests that we can only see change in relation to our habits. Giddens says that: 'We test our alternatives only in relation to the habits we have mastered. A life made out of just snapshots, a life without habit is a mindless experience'[92]. Religion gave us habit, at the very least.

Poetry gives us repetition too. I once heard a poet talk about the sonnet as a conversation with the past. She made the point that the form of the sonnet had remained unchanged since it was created, and that each time she wrote or read a sonnet she felt she was in conversation with its creator. The form repeats the content changes.

---

[92] Quote by Anthony Giddens. In *The Corrosion of Character* by Richard Sennett, 1998. W. W. Norton and Company.

So we can get a sense of the past through form and ritual, although our working lives have little of this that is valued. We consider repetition as rigidity, and the lack of ability to turn on a dime as a handicap in one's ability to progress up the ladder. To change jobs every couple of years is almost a necessity to demonstrate one's flexibility and ambition. We say we have 'stayed too long', when we spend 5 years in the same organisation.

Work with a favourite poem to learn the value of repetition
Find a poem you love, memorise it and spend 5 minutes of clock time in a quiet place repeating the poem to yourself.

We have little routine and repetition in our working lives bar the visits to recruitment consultants, and the sense of deja vu when filling in the same psychometric tests every couple of years. Routine can give us confidence to accept fragmentation, and can help us stop focusing only on the short-term. Routine can start to open up the possibility for acting now for future generations. All can start with a life that values routine as well as the unpredictable. I am reminded of my running time. I don't always go at the same time. I do, however, have a short route, a medium route and a long route. I map them out when I arrive at any place and choose one each day depending on my energy levels. There is a peace of mind that develops when you follow the same route time and time again. You get to know it intimately. There are times when I establish a routine that takes me through the same route at the same time, and then I can also benefit from getting to know the same people. I start to get recognised by people.

Leonard Koren talks about the tea ceremony in Japan commenting that repetition is after all the essence of tradition. '[The tea ceremony] has value as a meditation exercise. Non-thinking repetition of mechanical forms allows one to concentrate simply on being without the distraction of having to make decisions.' We can rest in routine. We have so little routine in lives that foreground only difference and change that we cannot find the peace of mind we are looking for. There are many uses for routine, such as the way that learning the

4. Making the most of time 137

lines of a play by rote helps the actor get into the depth of a given character.

Many of our modern rituals do not have the depth of the ones I have discussed. I once heard somebody say, when talking about wanting to leave America, that he had a desire to live in a country where there was more to ritual than snorting cocaine and paging your agent. There are ways in which the content of our forms and rituals does matter.

Angeles Arrien says we can become addicted to intensity, and that this can easily be demonstrated by those with a low tolerance for boredom: 'If things become too dull or routine, people who are addicted to intensity will dramatise, sensationalise and exaggerate their life experience in order to feel alive'. Our working lives are often the place where we play out this particular addictive pattern. We collude with each other to justify the value of change for its own sake, and diminish the need for continuity and routine because it allows us to feed our addiction to intensity.

Develop simple daily rituals

Pay attention to rituals you already do, and value them as teaching you about lived time. If you have not got many rituals, develop some. Remember you can rest in routine.

A simple ritual is using the same cup for your coffee each morning, a ritual highlighted by one of my interviewees. In a paper discussing coping strategies for chief executives in pressured environments, I read the following quote when discussing Hannah: 'But why, for instance, does she have to be well dressed before she can start the intercontinental tele-conference? Why does she always insist on having the same suite in her hotel? Why is it so important to her that she can rely on her local supermarket knowing her by the automated customers' system?' The paper stresses the importance of relying on certain rhythms. I become aware of what I call my 'little quirks' when I am away on business: the same hotel room, watching CNN on waking up (at hotels, never at home), the same restaurant and once I have found 'my' restaurant, I will also have a 'same' dish repeatedly.

I also have rituals when writing at home, and my day is often marked by the same events around me. I hear a car at 7.15, my neighbour's daughter arriving to leave her dogs at mum's before going to work; I hear 'the girls' (4 Jack Russell dogs) go out for their morning walk; I know my neighbours have lunch each day after the morning chores, and I often will pop in for a chat about then, this marks the end of my morning; I hear the dogs again at about 4.00 as they go out for their afternoon walk; I know I have been working too long when I see a torch light outside in the dark. It's the girls coming out for a last pee before going to bed. This is now time for me to switch off my computer and rest. The ongoing debate amongst scholars of time about the growing dominance of linear measured time, which drives out natural and social time and rhythms,[93] can easily be mapped onto our everyday experience. We just need to attend more to what repeats in our day-to-day experience, and understand the importance of this by creating and valuing our own rituals and routines.

What has Rap music got to do with time?
I noticed something whilst jogging in the countryside yesterday. I was enjoying the view and the silence, when I heard a thumping noise that got louder and louder as I approached a white van parked in a drive. Two young men were working in the garden and the thumping, regular, repetitive, rhythm was coming from the white van. They were listening to rap music. Maybe the popularity of this kind of music with young people has to do with the lack of structure and repetition in our lives. As a biological system we need different kinds of rhythm in our outer and inner lives, but the only rhythms in our lives nowadays tend to be 'go like hell' or 'stop', as my driving choices were described long ago. Maybe the sound of rap music meets a basic need for repetition in young people's lives.

---

[93] Axel Hounnschild in the journal *Time and Society*. A review of two books on lived time and against the hegemony of clock time: *Against Acceleration: Stopping and thinking for a new culture* by Peter Heintel, 1999 and *The body clock: Making use of natural rhythms and escaping non-stop pressure* by Jurgen Zulley and Barbara Knab, 2000. Peter Heintel is the founder of 'The Society for the Deceleration of Time' with 100 members at present. Vol. 10 (2/3): 401-406, 2001.

The past into the present: Developing a sense of place

We no longer attach value to having a sense of place. What is a sense of place? 'A sense of place is something we ourselves create in the course of time. It is the result of habit and custom.'[94] We commit to staying in one place over time. In a world that finds justification in abandoning whole communities because the economic imperative is such that it would be inefficient to subsidise them, it is hard to keep a practice of having or developing a sense of place to help us stay connected with our past. Aboriginal dreamtime has a sense of place, and it does not just connect the place with the living generation, but tells stories that connect particular mountains, unique rivers, and individual rocks to past generations. Yet we find it hard to understand how it is possible to stay in the same job for more than 5 years. We move to 'better' neighbourhoods, better jobs, better countries, and think nothing of leaving behind a sense of a place that may go back generations – we do this in the name of a better quality of life, often understood mainly through the measures of success in clock time – comfort and increased consumption.

We can start to re-develop a sense of place in quite simple ways. One way it is lost is by feeling that we have to have the best. So we drive miles to get to the best of anything, and getting the best not only takes time, but also dislocates us from our local community. However, we could base our lifestyle choices on physical closeness as well as having the best.

What is the best that is close?

Set a limit to how far you will travel for work, leisure, entertainment, etc. Once the limit is set, then find the best within that area.

It is easier to preserve a sense of place than it is to create one. We lead rushed lives within networks that lack spatial and temporal coherence, and we complain that we have to 'use' our time travelling

---

[94] In *A Sense of Place, a Sense of Time*' by John Brinckerhoff Jackson, 1994. Yale University Press.

to see family and friends – often to the exclusion of having time at home.[95] Because of these disjointed networks, we find that time at home has to be Taylorized – broken down and made efficient – in the same way as time at work. I say it is hard to re-create a lost sense of place because it may mean we have to make some tough decisions with relationships that matter in our lives. For example, perhaps you stop seeing that close friend who now lives too far away, or you no longer see family members who are still living where you were born, or you move back to your place of origin. These are tough decisions, but they would help you make the most of your time.

Once we have our place, we could stay in that place through the years. Again this is hard to do through the lens of clock time. We don't want to miss the chance of that better job, or that better house. A focus on lived time means that we add other criteria to our list. Will the job or the house give me the temporal lifestyle I want? Can I say that it will really be better to move and leave behind a sense of place built up through the years just to make more money? We expand our notion of 'better' to mean more than an increase in spending power. We look at this in the last chapter.

Some of us work hard to buy a house in the sun to retire to. Often our choice of location is based on a place we like as a holiday destination. We buy the house. We go on holidays to the house, and we do this regularly if we are lucky. We retire to it and find ourselves in a new community, where we often do not speak the language well, and miss our family and friends back home. We put up a for sale sign and go back home. A faulty sense of time led us to think that it was all just a matter of finding a beautiful property, but we ignore the web-work of life that sustains us. This is not about a dream house, but about people and places we know well.

The future into the present: Am I self-centred or is it just me?

There is evidence to suggest that we need to switch off the 'me-centres' of the brain to be able to find true rest. Andrew Newberg[96], a neuroscientist at the University of Pennsylvania, has studied the

---

[95] See 'Squeezing time' by D. Southerton in *Time and Society* Vol. 12,no.1, pp. 5-25 (2003).
[96] In 'In search of god'. *New Scientist*, 21 April, 2001.

neurobiology of religion for decades. His work is part of the new discipline of Neurotheology. His findings indicate that meditation helps us achieve this switching off of the 'me-centres'. Skilled meditators report a loss of their sense of self after they have been meditating for long periods. Newberg studied this phenomenon, and found that the parietal lobes are much less active in meditation, prayer and chanting than when just sitting. There is also an area said to regulate our sense of self in the brain – our self-image and the sense of space and time inhabited by the self- and this area also shows reduced activation in meditation. During the process the limbic system, seat of our emotions, is activated. Newberg argues that when we feel limbic activation and deactivation of the parietal lobes, we can have an experience of 'a sensed presence' or, in common terminology, an experience of God.

Other researchers in this area have concluded that we are hardwired to have an experience from time to time that gives us a sense of presence. We are hardwired to also have a rest from the self from time to time. Or, as James Hillman puts it, we are hardwired to pay ritual attention to something more than the altar of self. A focus on God and religion gives us that, but most of us do not have religion as a central part of our lives anymore. This may explain why we continue to pursue new-age religions, and why cults are still so popular in western society.

We are starved of the need to take a rest from ourselves. If we don't know that this is a basic expectation for humans, it is hard to seek it out when not motivated by a spiritual search. We don't know what we don't know. It is possible that in letting go of religion we have damaged the balance there used to be between 'me' and 'other' in our world. We seek peace of mind in our self-serving aims and are ignorant that the place to find it lies elsewhere, in letting go of our selves, giving those parietal lobes a rest, and switching off the 'self' centres in the brain. If humans need an external frame of reference that connects us from our past to our present and to our future, but have lost it, this could help explain our need to find meaning at work, more often than outside of it. Work may be the only external frame of reference we have left – we can dedicate ourselves to the goals of the organisation we belong to.

Thou who liveth within my heart
Awaken me to the immensity of thy spirit
To the experience of thy living presence
Deliver me from the bonds of desire
From the slavery of small aims
From the delusion of narrow egohood

Suffuse me with the incandescence of thy love
Which includes and embraces the darkness
Like the light that surrounds the dark core of the flame
Like the love of a mother that surrounds
The growing life in the darkness of her womb
Like the earth protecting the tender germ of the seed

Let me be the seed of thy living light
Give me the strength to burst the sheath of selfhood
So that I may awaken to the greater life
To the all-embracing life of love.
A Buddhist prayer[97]

To bring the future back to our present we could start today projects the results of which we will not live to see. Like the farmers who would plant acorns for future generations, or the oak forest planted by the Swedish government which was harvested recently after being planted 150 years ago by people who had a sense of time. We resolve to start acting today for future generations, even though we do not know what will happen. This may leads us to a different 'now' than the kind of 'now' that says 'act only for today'.

Religion used to teach us how to live beyond our front door, but we have little secular guidance today and have retreated to the safety of the shopping mall. We put the individual at the centre and all else loses value. A healthy sense of time asks that we learn to live with the humility of this statement: 'To have started anything is much too big a claim for anyone to make, at most we have a small part to play

---

[97] Used in the meditation practices of the Friends of the Western Buddhist Order.

in life'. I overheard this on the radio. Somebody who had achieved a great deal, and yet had the awareness to know that he was not the centre of his universe said it. I wish I had caught his name.

⏳

Pema Chodron's Opinion spotting[98]

'One of the best practices for everyday living is to notice our opinions. We could begin to notice our opinions just as we notice that we are thinking when we are meditating. This is an extremely helpful practice because we have a lot of opinions, and we tend to take them as truth. We can begin to notice them and we can label them as opinions. All ego really is, is our opinions'

We know what we want. We can plan for our small aims. To give ourselves over to the unknown and allow ourselves to attend to what life wants from us rather than what we want from it, as Victor Frankl used to say, is hard. Particularly for individuals driven by the clock, and by a society that puts the individual above the collective in all manner of things. We have difficulty in grasping the sentiment of abandonment to life expressed in this poem[99]: 'it is possible that somewhere down in the depths my boat has struck against a great thing. And nothing happens. Nothing happens. Rocks, wave, water. Nothing happens. Or, has everything happened and are we standing now in the new country?' David Whyte tells us, 'we are not supposed to work out what our calling is, we are supposed to give tremendous attention to the world and the world will tell us what our calling is'. We feel our ego shrinking at the thought of letting go of its decision making power. He quotes Wordsworth to make this point:

'Oh, Dear friend,
to the brim my heart was full;
I made not vows
But vows were made for me;

---

[98] In *When Things Fall Apart*, 1997. Shambala Publications.
[99] Quoted by David Whyte in 'Poetry and the imagination'. Sounds True Recordings. www.soundstrue.com

Bond unknown to me was given
That I should be a dedicated spirit,
And on I walked in blessedness
That even yet remains.'[100]

Wordsworth experiences this after a walk in the woods full of deep attention. Whyte says we attend, listen to the world for what must be done, attend to our imagination, trust ourselves to delve into the depths of it and then come back with a communal gift. After all, any exploration of life is about achieving a 'private understanding, which is then made communal by your craft'. We write our understanding to give back to our world, we paint it, or we speak it. Whatever we choose to do the cycle is not complete until we give back. In this he echoes Joseph Campbell's Hero's journey: 'A hero ventures forth from the world of common day into a region of supernatural wonder: Fabulous forces are encountered and a decisive victory is won.' Campbell then says that the hero returns from this mysterious adventure with the power to bestow boons on his fellow man.

Martin Luther King is quoted as saying that every citizen has a responsibility to be able to answer the question: 'What am I prepared to die for?' When I asked this of a close friend he said the answer was easy, in this generation we die for the right to party. To develop a sense of our future, and set goals that reflect the whole of time, maybe we need to revisit our personal answer to that question. We need a coherent thread to connect the past with the present and the future; a narrative of life that defines who we are as something more than somebody with the ability to keep becoming something, or someone else, depending on the needs of somebody's self-serving goals. This will give us back our place in the world, and the understanding that time is life.

---

[100] Amended extract from 'The Prelude' by William Wordsworth.

Take time to think about a future
When was the occasion of your longest view? Write about a future you want, but which you will not be alive to see. Maybe after you write choose to do a little action today the result of which you will not live to see.

A life with a healthy sense of time – David

David was never tempted by the promises of clock time living. He never got on the treadmill, so never had to re-learn how to get off it. His success in life cannot be measured with the instruments of clock time. I learnt about David through a conversation about this book with a colleague. She said she knew somebody of our age group who had made very different choices. He lived in a small village, and had shunned modern life in order to embrace lived time, though he would not describe his life like this. I was keen to interview him. He was from an area in England where professionals working in the city of London also lived. They used the village as a bedroom town, but were not originally from the village. I feel enriched and enlivened by having met David, but most of all I feel humbled by the profound appreciation of life that he has. The fact that he was willing to open up and talk to me, a stranger, made me feel privileged.

He started talking about his background and childhood in the village: In those days, he said 'hundreds of blokes, lived and worked in the village so they did not have to go anywhere else...we used to go walking for miles, and then once I did not take enough provisions with me and got lost...it is just discovering your youth and your strength of character...and it is character building, see?'

Mariana (MF): Because there were things here in the village, you had everything you wanted...

David (D): ... yeah, you discovered it yourself, play in the woods, making dams, it is just natural because you are in tune with nature, and you appreciate what is around you, and I've never been one really for drinking and things like that...so I've never been in a gang of chaps...years ago. I've never been drawn by it all. I tried all these things but never really took to it, it would be so easy as an individual to take to these things, but that is an easy way out; you just discover so many other good things, that's the truth of it.

MF: And you've never been tempted to go anywhere else...

D: At 15 I left school and I was doing work for Peter, helping in the coal run. He has seen me grow up. I would think nothing of it, opening up paths, digging ditches or whatever, it had to be done, and helping Peter with bridges and things...but again it's just so fulfilling... the thing is that you are doing things, and you look back at what you have done, you were achieving things each day, it's just achievements that people are going to see in years and years to come and repairing things what people don't do no more, repairing things. Things are just let go, like ditches and things, well things have changed, people don't have the time no more...it has to be instant now or nothing

MF: The interesting thing to me is that you managed to make a living whilst staying in the context of your community, whereas those you have called the 'professionals' have left in search for more money...

D: Years ago you saw more men with dinner bags when I was a kid than you do now. Now they go in the shop, because they don't get time to do it. With all the modern things now, the majority of people have not got time to sit with things like making a sandwich and flask. It's instant, everything, 'cause they have not got time. But I fail to believe. If they have not got time, they must have a bottle they are putting their time in for later life, they are saving it (smiling). My granny said, I used to hear her clock and mow the grass for her with an old push mower, which I still use, she always said "you know that old clock will be there well past when I'm gone". And now, whenever I hear that clock chiming, I'm 2 years off 50 now, I hear it and sigh, it is now 18 years since she died, 88 years young. Now I am listening to that clock...and you realise that old clock still goes at the same pace and it is valuing your time to make time for the things you enjoy. I always think you got to appreciate the time of your own playtime. Earn your money to enjoy your own quality time.

MF: You made a decision that you were not going to keep going for more and more...because you wanted to maintain your quality of life...

D: I have learnt a lot from the past. I hope it never leaves me as long as I live, and the demands of modern life I hope do not catch up with me.

MF: Because you realise the negative consequences of it?

D: Yes, I realise the lesser contentment you have. You hardly hear anybody singing, or whistling, like they used to. I know times have changed ...but there is that grim look on people's faces of fear because, they have not discovered that...I say this more than anything in the world: You work to live. But it is to do with money. It is greed in a sense. Massive greediness. And they don't get pleasure from their work, we do because we see what we've done and we've done it for years. It is a modern disease, greediness.

MF: Yes. As you said earlier it is hard to change when 'you are already part of the 'jigsaw puzzle'.

D: I think it is just so sad because they don't discover peace, and then I realise that 1 in 4 people are having treatment for nerve trouble today because the pace they are living at, it's getting faster and faster, and more of them are going to psychologists to try and sort them out and they go on these breaks that are to do with having treatment for peace. But either it is there or it isn't.

MF: How come that you were never tempted by big cars...how come that you were able to see through to the fact that it does not give people peace...that people just have to keep earning more and more to keep up...

D: (Smiling). I always kept my life simple, as to what my capacity can cope with. So therefore, I discovered other things. I watched and I learned from other people, and I'll think something is not right here... and I'll pick up on it. If you sit by a river that is peace to your brain because we are 70/80 % water, so you listen to a river and that is peaceful. We have to live by water because we need water in life, and if you are near the elements of nature what provides for us, you will not go far wrong on what you want in life. And I can sit there by the river 'cause of the fishing and that, and that's our lifeline, water. And that is peace.

If you feel that sometimes you've taken up too much work, and sometimes I do, I think 'I must get to that, I must get that finished...' I say hang on, I'm starting to chase here. And if you work hard enough for a few days, you need that day to do what you always wanted to in life – go walk by the bluebells, and sit there, listen to the birds in the morning, or that river that takes me back to so many generations, I always think of Tim (somebody who is now dead), I always think of him fishing, and I will never forget that for as long as I live. That is part of me that I never want to forget for as long as I live.

MF: not just the river but also what it means to you, your family, your memories. You remember the past and remember people who are not around anymore

D: and them woods with voices, laughing children playing ...but they don't now. They just use it as a garbage pile, it is becoming a very big dump, the countryside, for chucking stuff about...coke bottles, washing machines. I enjoyed water, paddling in there, and you used to spend all day there and get in trouble because you were late for your dinner. My mother would send a party out, and I'd been making a dam up in the creek. Things are different now. But years ago you were very safe, but everyone worried about each other a bit more years ago, because it had more value, the human ways.

MF: I wonder...In your example earlier of the people waiting for a train at 6 in the morning and you watch them, what made them leave the place they too once must have had...

D: They forget. They lost their identification somewhere along the rat race...If you lived in a town for several generations you know no better. See? And every 5 years things are getting faster, and getting more ratty, people pushing each other and ...go into any supermarket and it is like a cattle market, and that is just to get food, and the baskets are full up like it's the end of the world what I think will happen one day 'cause less and less people on the land providing, the land will be there in years and years to come, but there wont be many people able to work it because there won't be any understanding. I'm very lucky of those in my generation I'm still in the village, a lot of my generation have moved on because financially they could not afford to stay in the village.

MF: I would imagine that you too could be greedy, you have your own house in the village

D: Of course and sell it for a fortune, or rent it out and move into some rented accommodation...but I wouldn't, I have spent the hours here, I have feelings for the village, and what little feeling there is left here I always stick with forever. That is why I have so many people on film, what I relate too (he films and interviews people in the village) and I relate very little to what the future is, I don't find it very tasteful. I love to discover new people, there is only 1 in 50 that is worth knowing because of the speed they are living at, they are not even in tune. Or understand each other.

MF: ...like you say they are rushing around so much looking for contentment and peace they are not realising that they need to stop to find it

D: ...Well, the ones that is giving them treatment for tension and the like, need something done for themselves, they have bigger problems than who they are curing...I might be wrong, but it seems to me some of them need help themselves because they are working so many hours to try to help others that they have loopholes in their own problems.

D: I talk to old people in the village because I like the past in a way better than I do the future. Because it's the achievements what people did years ago, I find that the pace of what people are achieving now it is just nothing, it is just their own empires, that is the truth of it and I don't find that very inspiring.

MF: Instead of doing things for the community?

D: ...Well, just helping each other. It's gone because of the empires to individuality. It is sort of what I call 'telephone people' – hello and goodbye in the same breath. It is getting involved. They don't want to get themselves involved, in case they might have to do something, like take the washing in for somebody. It is just recognising each other and caring. It is gradually going and it's quite distasteful in some ways, modern life. I still think that a lot of people come to submission, that is why things will shrink as time goes on because there will be less and less people to talk to who would want to bother to talk to each other.

MF: ...because people just resign themselves to the fact that it is so hard to go against the tide?

D: ...And I think you will find that as time goes on the islands will get smaller and smaller. Unless something happens to change our direction, it will get worse and worse. What there is left in the village, it's lovely to meet people you know, it is real nice to recognise a face, amongst all the faces, I always think.

MF: that is why it is important to you to preserve the past?

D: That is why I have so many people on tape because they put into life in a morning, what people will not put in 6 months now. You just can't...you have to accept modern living. I don't think it will ever come back, what was, to be honest with you.

MF: Are there any negative consequences...how difficult is it to stick to your guns and put your quality of life before anything else?

D: I don't aspire to any big car, big house...

MF: How do people who come new in the village treat you?

D: They don't speak.

MF: What do you do now for work?

D: I work on the bread van now. I deliver bread in the early hours, I start at something like 1.30 and finish by 9.30, a few hours sleep before and after and then I go out and do my own work that I enjoy back on the land. Plus it's more active. I have never had such a comfortable job in my life, delivering bread. Not like sitting in an office, but still. I modernised, but not really because it is still the old-fashioned way they do the bread, my mother's ancestors used to run the shop in the 1920's. So it is almost like I am following in the footsteps of a lot of my relatives...it is almost a spiritual thing, so I follow along...and every so often...when I get myself a bit edgy...I go to the cemetery to cool myself down and realise why I'm here, and I walk around and talk to everybody along there every so often, just to realise, well, you know, it is only a short thread of time and the dividing line (between life and death) is so thin that you have to enjoy everyday like your last day, 'cause I'll be right one day. Whatever time you are, because it is only a number. I realise something watches all this anyway, it is all an experiment really life, it is enjoying everyday, and making the most of it, and that is the truth of it.

MF: and never getting so focused on results that...

D: the only results is what's on the ground, what grows out of the ground and enjoying what is around and enjoying your surrounding for what 's been provided. 'Cause one day ain't like the next, there is always something different in each day to see, flowers coming out in the spring, there is always something, how people get bored I just don't know...we all come to saturation point, wondering what we are doing...but then you pick yourself up, sometimes you take on too much, but that is called life really. But that is for your brain to tell you: hang on a minute you are working too hard now, you are overstepping...then you go to the river or to the cemetery, back to where your roots are...the people who are getting on that train in the morning don't have that to go back to...no. They have a blank. It is just a way of making money. They have to do it because they've lived like it so long that they got to...it is materialistic, a lot of it is, they could easily make do with a lot less, but I don't know if they could cope with a lot less, it is discipline.

I'm not against drink or smoking, but the thing is having discipline for the things you like ...every so often I buy myself some cigars and I sit on the seat by the green and have a cigar, and then I pack it in for months and months.... and then I see people in pubs...drinking, smoking, it is like a circus and everyone is trying to be the clown...but I sit on that seat outside, and I take sandwiches, I make myself a picnic and sit on that seat that dad used to sit on, and many others and Mr C. who was the cobbler. When I was a kid he donated 30 years of his time, but now you look at it, and it just means nothing what people do in the amount of time, it is just like this (snap finger). A 5-minute wonder is worth more than somebody's 30 years. It does not got no value and I look at that and I think when he used to be in that shoe shop, looking at shoes, or repairing them, I used to spend quite a bit of time just to chat to him. It all comes back to me like it has never left me, and I got to recognise the past to survive for the future.

MF: What does time mean to you?

D: Time is ever so precious because I know each day it's getting less. I know it is old to think that. But you have to think you will. You have to think everyday is a bonus. And sometimes you have grim days but you have to have grim days to appreciate good days. Time is not lacking but precious. I always think there is so much to discover. 'Cause I do love travelling, going to other countries. There is not enough time to do everything we want to...so much to discover and so little time to do it in. You have to pace yourself, 'cause you can't do everything. When you do get time to go and discover somewhere...I don't always want to come back because I am so intrigued with other cultures... I get quite absorbed, I don't always want to come back... and yet sometimes you wonder what you got back from other cultures when you get back... but there is nothing like home, the roots do draw you back.

I think that with the immense amount of money that one can earn these days, why people work so much in the way of the rat race, when there is other good qualities of having somewhere nice to be that they want to be...but they never get to that point...because they never discipline themselves to put that time aside. And you have to put time aside to do things you enjoy, it is not good later on because, it is probably too late, it's count down. I put time aside for holiday, and if I want extra money I work, when I don't want extra money I don't work. See? So long as I have enough money for bills and food there is nothing else I really want. Just normal living. I smile everyday, I am lucky, I am alive, I hear the birds, I enjoy now, enjoy the good people I know, and it is lovely to see faces. It is like flowers, really. Opening up. You have to make time for what you enjoy.

And at the end of the day, I know I am not missing out on anything. Not everybody would want to live like me. Nothing makes me wish I had my life again. Not good dreaming what you want to do if you don't do it. I must admit I have always fulfilled all mine. Discovering yourself and going for it. We are lucky, I suppose. But I made my own luck. I have good health, and I do appreciate that. Looking after mother and father with their problems when they declined, it gave me inspiration. Well, I stayed at home until I was 30 taking care of them. So I helped them and it stopped me being selfish, and even now I love giving up time for other persons. But I feel as if I achieved something if I can give to others. It gives you so much.

D: We are moulded to a certain way of life. And people are losing the meaning of life. I am very lucky for somebody in my age group, to be firm in my standing about how I feel. Understanding yourself and being contented with your self that you can give to others – the meaning of life. You do have to recharge yourself 'cause sometimes you can give too much, people can live off your electricity 'cause some people haven't got it. If I was cut tomorrow, I have done everything I ever wanted to in life. There is nothing I want for. Bills paid, good food, good bed to sleep in, good friends, what more could I want.

David lives his life very much in the I-Thou mode of being. He has a focus that is beyond himself, he has the existential coherence that comes from not ever having bought into the grand deception that his life was his alone. He finds his place in the world in relation to others and nature, he lives the idea of reciprocal participation in the world. The river speaks to him, his ancestors speak to him, the future speaks to him and he knows that his purpose is to be the words of the earth, as David Abram so eloquently put it. His goals and dreams are grounded in his sense of lived time. He is not in love with himself taking care of old people. He merely reflects 'if I get the opportunity to do something for somebody else that gives me so much'.

He lives the correct life, as defined in previous chapters, a life according to biological expectations. He has never lost his ground, and his dreams are not of himself as leader, but of himself as someone who listens to the questions that life is asking. He does not have the arrogance that I have, of imagining that he has the right to ask what he wants from life and get it at any cost.

Through my meeting with David I learnt that it was possible to be part of our world and live in time and not by the clock. That the choices we have to make are tough ones, but that we cannot blame anything but our drive for comfort and consumption for not having the peace of mind we want right now. It would have been a lot more self-justifying to start to judge David and his choices. You may be doing that right now. He was not educated, in the sense of having a profession, and he did not have any of the outward signs of somebody who counts in our world. He was just stuck in the past. He should get a life. You may be thinking some of those things and others that deny the value of what he and people like him have to teach us professionals. It is your choice not to listen. My wish is that if you are tempted to dismiss him, you question your own virtue: What if you are wrong?

In a sense it was easy for David, he had been smart enough never to let go of what gave meaning to his life. He had stood firm in his conviction that there was something wrong with a way of life the left people with grim faces and terrified of getting involved in case they might have to do something for others. The rest of us are not so lucky. We thought that comfort and consumption would give us more...it has certainly given us more to live with, but maybe not much to live for. David seems to have applied his healthy time sense to making choices that are congruous with his health and wellbeing.

A few more stepping stones to a healthy sense of time

⌛

All the time in the world

Tell at least one person in your day that you have all the time in the world and notice their responses. As you engage in these conversations you will start to notice your own assumptions about time, in particular you will see how attached we all are to believing that not having enough time says something about how important and/or successful we are to others.

⌛

The not-to-do list

Ask yourself each morning 'What isn't going to happen today?' And as you create this list notice how it makes you feel. You may learn that what does not happen in our day is often that which we would most want to happen.

⌛

The magic wand

Ask yourself 'if I knew I had all the time in the world, what would I be worrying about today?' If time is not an issue, you may notice some of the root causes for your lack of peace of mind today. If you had a magic wand that gives you time then you may see that there are real problems that need addressing, and that will never be dealt with if your focus is on finding time.

⌛

4. Making the most of time 155

One step too far[101]

Find one item of material culture within your home that has undergone considerable "development" since it was first introduced, e.g. refrigerator, knife, washing machine. Take the time to trace the stages of development of this device over the years. If you do not know, do some research at your local library and find out. Your aim is to identify the point in the device's development where no more improvement to function was made.

The Desert Island without disks

You are alone in a tropical Island. You are Tom Hanks in 'Castaway', but your aim is not to get home. You are home. Write down as many activities as you can to 'plan' your day. Now the island transforms into a place where you are still alone but you can now spend money for activities. You have £100 to spend. Write down the activities you would add to your day.

Pick the longest queue

When you go to the supermarket walk up and down looking for your queue, but – only for a week – yours will be the longest you can find. What can you learn about your lack of patience? What can you do with the extra time spent in that queue? How many ways can you find to breathe in the impatience of the world and breath out infinite time for all?

A conversation without me

Have a conversation with a close colleague or friend where you do not

---

[101] From Mark H. Burch in *Simplicity*, 1995. New Society Publishers.

use the words: I, me, mine or my. Notice how it changes your frame of reference and makes you perceive yourself as part of something bigger than just an isolated self.

⌛

Name your year

Try creating a personal calendar. Reflect on your yearly cycle and name your months. Do your months last 30 days? What are they called? How many are there? How do you know it is the beginning of your year, and how do you know it is the end? Reflect your lifestyle in your naming. What will the names tell your great-grandchildren about the kind of person you were?

⌛

Wean yourself off the clock

Plan and 'live' a week as if the smallest division in your clock was an hour. You can only arrange meetings on the hour, or phone calls or anything. The smallest chunk possible in this week is the hour. So, if you have to be there at 5.00 and you want to be on time you have to plan to be there at 4.00. The value of scheduling like this is that you will never rush again. However, you will also be unable to do as many activities as you do now. Notice what this does to your time perception and your working life.

A PHILOSOPHY OF TIME

Lived Time

> *'I understand that my time is truly my time. And even though the pace of my life, like everyone else's, is often directed by the world around me, it has become clear that people have considerably more control over their tempos than they often let themselves believe. And I have come to see another basic truth: that our time is our life. How we construct and use our time defines the texture and quality of our existence.'*
> Robert Levine[102]

The most all-pervading idea in our understanding of time is that time *is* Money. The world of clock time living is fundamentally structured by the idea that time is a limited resource that can run out, that has to be saved, that can be sold, that can be wasted, that has to be managed. In clock time we do not listen to our inner rhythms, and because of this we have developed a faulty sense of time; one that favours surface and quantity, and not depth and quality. We are starved of meaning, and keep looking for it in our time management systems. I quoted Edward Luttwak[103] in the introduction: 'Whatever is worthwhile about us, as individuals, groups and societies is the inefficient part. Inefficiency is where human life exists, social life exists, where love, hatred and culture exist'. We keep looking for efficiency in clock time living at our peril, as we are certainly not going to find peace of mind there.

The choice between clock time and lived time seems quite stark. The 'better' choice is 'obviously' lived time. Yet we continue to reify time through the clock. Our working lives are run and driven by clock time, not lived time. We wake up thinking: 'Am I late?' 'What's the time?' We order our relationships through the time we have available: 'I can only give you 5 minutes.' Time is not an issue anymore, because there is none. All that remains is the option to use our lack of time as an index of how powerful and successful we are. In short, we say we want to find time to do that which satisfies, but keep finding ourselves with less and less time to even complete our must-do-list.

This book has asked some tough questions about the underlying

---

[102] In *A Geography of Time*, 1997. Basic Books.
[103] *Turbo Capitalism – winners and losers in the global economy* by Edward Luttwak, 1999. Harper Collins.

causes for the flawed sense of time that is clock time. I recognise clock time gives us many opportunities to achieve, but question the value of taking the metaphor so literally that it becomes our only perception. The metaphor has limitations, and in highlighting certain things it obscures others. Our sense of time is flawed in clock time because we are failing to perceive these limitations, and we continue to insist the solution to our pressured lifestyles lies in more of the same. It is not working for us now, but we believe that if we keep doing the same thing it will work for us eventually.

A healthy sense of time is lived time. Lived time brings time back to our body and our experience. Lived time is time that makes sense, time that works with our human concerns, not against them. We can make the most of time by learning that there is life beyond clock time. We can learn to have genuine choice, and be truly multitemporal. We can develop a healthy sense of time. When we do, we can stop asking for ways to maintain our work-life balance, and start to act in the world today according to our desired temporal lifestyle. We can start to make not only lifestyle choices, but also genuine temporal choices. Making the most of our time is possible. We have to commit to a lifetime of practice to learn how to relate to time beyond the clock. If each day we turn up, attend to our breath, note our opinions, and choose to relate to a moment with deep attention, then we are making the most of our time.

It really can be that simple. We have taken the time out of things so much that we live in times when: 'the fresh creation of meaning has become a rare occurrence, a time when people speak in ready-made conventional ways...a time when meaning has become impoverished', as Abram told us in previous chapters. If we keep searching for ways in which clock time can take the time out of things even more, we will continue to impoverish our lives. We will keep doing more with less and less. If we do this, then less of the inefficiencies that make life worth living will remain part of our lives. If we want to resolve the paradox between our time and our life we must look at reversing this equivalence, and choose to live our lives by taking things out of time. So our mantra is no longer: 'how I can do more in less time?' Our question has become: *'how can I do less in more time?* Just that simple question has the power to change our personal world and the whole world. With this question as a guide, the number of things we do daily is reduced. This means we can't work as much, we can't keep as many balls up in the air, and we can no longer be proud of our complicated life.

> *'I do have a complicated life, which requires organising to work, in terms of looking after my kids, my work, my friends, in terms of what I am doing. I spend quite a bit of time organising that... so when I talked about this day, the immediate context is the next few weeks, which I know are going to be very busy. And one reason I know that is because I was talking to somebody last night arranging when we might meet, and I did not have an opportunity until 5 weeks from now. Which quite shocked me, it is like everything is ordained in terms of what I have to do. And it is not as if the things that I have to do are unpleasant, they are all things that I am pleased to be doing. I just don't like it when there is no slack time...it is not like there is no free time, because one of those things is that I am going away with my parents for their wedding anniversary...that will be a relaxed time. But it is still time set aside. I know what I am doing. The way that this rhythm of life starts to work is that I finish teaching, and then at the end of that I drive to the Isle of Wight, and then drive back home. I may not even drive back home, 'cause I then have to go to Copenhagen, so I then have to drive straight to the airport. Go to Copenhagen for 2 days, I come back from Copenhagen...if I am lucky I catch the earlier flight...and then there is a breath of relief. I have reclaimed some time. So I might then get back home earlier, I then have a full evening, before I am away again for the next 3 days.'*
>
> An interviewee[104]

With this question: *'how can I do less in more time?'* as my guide, I simplify life and quite simply do less. The solution seems deceptively simple, and yet it is very complex. Bodil Jonson distinguishes between that which is complex and that which is complicated. The complicated we can at times simplify like a tangled skein of yarn. She suggests that

---

[104] From my formal interviews for this book.

5. A philosophy of time

it is good to simplify the complicated because we can then use it. Our lives can sometimes be complicated, and can benefit from being simplified. This might allow us to have a complex relationship to time instead of a complicated relationship to life.

Time is not complicated but complex, and we cannot make the assumption that something that is complex can be simplified. The complex, says Jonson, can be compared to a weaving, and: 'if you pull threads from a weaving, you ruin both its pattern and form. It is the same with time. Only respect for its complexity will get you anywhere.'[105] She concludes that simplifications simply aren't worth the trouble. If we apply her advice to theories of time that teach us that it is possible through human action to cheat time, we quickly realise that such theories just aren't worth the effort. For no matter how often you check on the olives, they just won't ripen any faster.[106] It is that complex; we just have to do fewer things and take more time to do them.

Most of this book has been about just how tough that is. We need an understanding of our relationship to time, we need to develop a new vocabulary for relating to time and, above all, we need courage to stand up for what we believe in.[107] It is our lack of decisiveness and courage that has kept us looking at the 'time' side of the equation rather than the 'things' side of the equation. Of course, in starting to look at the 'things' side of the equation we come face to face with our greediness. I call these confrontations 'Julia Roberts moments', as when in the film 'Pretty Woman' she turns down the offer of a luxury apartment and has the courage to risk losing it all rather than compromise her sense of what is right. Such moments face us daily. Often we accept the metaphorical apartment rather than risk any loss. We compromise our values and dreams for the short-term vision of having more materially. And we justify our actions as necessary, given that we have to earn money to live.

We looked at ways to develop a healthy time sense in the previous chapter. In this chapter I want to look at the weaving of time, a philosophy of time beyond clock time. I am going back to fundamental

---

[105] *Unwinding the Clock* by Bodil Jonson, Harcourt, 2001.
[106] Ibid Page 31.
[107] Ibid. Page 111.

principles, to philosophy and other disciplines, to start to formulate a different way of talking about our relationship to time, one that moves us beyond the clock.

When we talked about lived time in chapter 3 we looked at the phenomenological view of time, a time that makes sense, which has the body at its centre. Not the body as a memorial to the Me Generation, but the body as part of the web-work of the world. We explored how Abram sees the imagination as something we need to understand, as it is the link between sensation and reality. We are able to make the virtual real through our imagination. This is our greatest gift, and potentially our greatest weakness. This is what we do when we take the abstract idea that time is money and make it real in the way we choose to live.

Abram believes that our own signs have stifled us. We read marks on the page and visit websites. We sit on our comfortable chairs, in an environment that is climate controlled, isolated from our communities, creating a world in our minds of what was once done in the tangible life-world. This has allowed us to elaborate on the world and make our existence more comfortable, but at the cost of our ability to work well and live well. I am appealing to our enlightened self-interest to make us look beyond clock time. Abram's argument clearly tells us that the menu is not the food, and that our lack of peace of mind has to do with the inherently unsatisfying nature of having a life that is almost completely lived through our own signs and products.

Husserl's[108] view of time will help us here. For him, there is a level of time that is out there, external to us, which he calls transcendent time; one that is internal to us, which he calls immanent time; and one that is foundational – a time-constituting flow. He is fascinated by the fact that our 'now' is always changing and yet we are always conscious of what is just past. He looks at the fundamental features of time. How do we know that an object is a temporal object? We know it because it endures, therefore time has duration; we know it because the duration is specific, therefore time is concrete; we know

---

[108] *On the Phenomenology of the Consciousness of Internal Time.* Edmund Husserl (translated by J. B. Brough), 1991. Kluwer Academic Publishers.

it because the object has a temporal location, it is anchored to a place in time, therefore time has individuality. He also notes that a feature of a temporal object is that it has a mode of appearance – it could appear to us in the past, the present or the future.

He believes that the present has a privileged status as a point of orientation for the other modes. That it is a saddleback between past and future, as William James once commented. The past and the future always fringe the 'now', and without a sense of past and future we can have no sense of temporality.

Husserl also talks about the oneness of time. There are 3 aspects to the oneness of time: our sense of succession – all we experience has a unique place on a metaphorical time line. In this sense time is fixed and all we can do is experience the unique points on the line as slipping further away into the past. Next is our sense of simultaneity – each time point in our time line is a unity, the common form where many events can co-occur, so the same 'now' can contain many different events occurring at 'the same time'. Finally, there is the oneness of immanent and transcendent time – the time it takes a hawk to fly from A to B is the same time that it takes me to see the hawk flying from A to B. This may be an element of the oneness of time that we violate in the way we live now. Everything external to us seems to be moving at a speed that is much faster than our ability to perceive it in its completeness.

One of his theories regards time as a perceptual phenomenon; our ability to hear, see and feel determines our consciousness of time. If you attend to your visual field, you can 'see' time. Fixing on a point, you will see the content of the image change. That change is time. He proposes that there are actually more than 3 modes of time appearing to us:

- Secondary Past – what we normally call 'the past'
- Retention – our perception of objects as elapsing or as 'just having been'.
- Now
- Protention – our primary expectation of objects as arriving into our now
- Secondary Future – what we normally call 'the future'

With this view he gives us a sense of the past and the future as existing in the now, and of time as grounded in our perception of the world. This is a philosophy of lived time, and together with Abram's view, it reinforces the idea of time as embedded in perception and the body.

Abram thinks that once stories could be written down they could be separated from the physical places where the events in the stories happened. The place used to be the memory trigger for the stories to be told, but once they were written down the triggers became marks on paper: 'the inked traces left by the pen as it traverses the page replacing the earthly traces left by the animals, and one's ancestors, in their interactions with the local land.' In this sense we became able to abstract space and time. We could freeze time and read a snapshot of time over and over again. Linear detached time became possible as we removed ourselves from the land that gave us the cyclical grounded nature of time.

In this way, the connection between what we are doing right now and what our ancestors did in the past became severed. Myths and stories told orally carried the past into the present, and it was important to perform those stories with the same precision and care that had been applied by many previous generations. As Abram puts it: 'Employing the very phrases and gestures disclosed in mythic time, one actually becomes the ancestral being and thus rejuvenates the emergent order of the world'. In other words, by repeating activities from our past, we can bring the past back to life in our present.

Abram argues that in oral cultures, the experience of the world is one of the world continuously retelling itself, and that the unprecedented and singular have no place in cycling stories. In the past we attended to that which repeated itself, and not to that which was singular. We had a sense of the rhythms and the stability of life as a flow from past to present to future, and not a sense of the events that create discontinuity in that flow.

But once we write things down: 'a new experience of the permanence, fixity and unrepeatable quality' of events is established. We lose our sense of the flow of time with nature and gain (sic) a: 'new awareness of an irreversible and rectilinear progression of itemised events'. The possibility of clock time is born at this point, and our sense of time, as grounded in location and nature, starts to become faulty. Yet even today we are unable to talk about time without using our sense of bodies in space (see chapter 3). Our attention, however, starts to shift to events that are unique and without precedent, and these begin to be interpreted as the will of God. We develop a sense of time as a non-repeating sequence. Abram suggests that our loss of peace of mind can be traced back to this rupture between place and time, which came with writing and the alphabetic system. We have lost our sense of the cyclical recurring events of the earth, which marked the root of our understanding of time. With the Greeks, who refined alphabetic writing and further ruptured place and time, time becomes that which can be counted, clock time.

With clock time a thread of life no longer unites our notion of past and future. Abram comments that past and future have become almost independent realms that hold our attention as if they existed autonomously, without link to our now. We seem to have a compulsion to hang on to the past and plan for the future, trying to know them and yet not finding a way in. We are scared to death of what has now become the unknown. His argument is that the way in lies in re-learning our awareness of the life of the land, and yet he sees those around him cutting themselves off more and more from this in the name of comfort.

'There is a useful exercise that I devised back then to keep myself from falling completely into the civilised oblivion of linear time. You are welcome to try it the next time you are out of doors. I locate myself in a relatively open space; a low hill is particularly good, or a wide field. I relax a bit, take a few breaths, gaze around. Then I close my eyes, and let myself begin to feel the whole bulk of my past, the whole mass of events leading up to this very moment. And I call into awareness, as well, my whole future all those projects and possibilities that lie waiting to be realised. I imagine this past and this future as two vast balloons of time, separated from each other like the bulbs of an hourglass, yet linked together at the single moment where I stand pondering them. And then, very slowly, I allow both of these immense bulbs of time to begin leaking their substance into this minute moment between them, into the present. Slowly, imperceptibly at first, the present moment

begins to grow. Nourished by the leakage from the past and the future the present moment swells in proportion as those other dimensions shrink. Soon it is very large; and the past and future have dwindled down to mere knots on the edge of this huge expanse. At this point I let the past and the future dissolve entirely. And I open my eyes...

The unshakeable solidity of this experience is curious indeed. It seems to have something to do with the remarkable affinity between this temporal notion that we term "the present", and the spatial landscape in which we are embedded.'

David Abram[109]

This exercise has the potential to bring our life back to life, and give us a powerful experience of a healthy sense of time, a time that (literally) makes sense. Our separation of things and time is simply counter to our direct pre-conceptual experience. Abram believes that his way of creating a living present where the past and future dissolve in the present moment opens up a way to a healthy time sense. He believes that he has opened up the way for the: 'gradual rediscovery of the past and the future – no longer as autonomous mental realms, but now as aspects of the corporeal present, of this capacious terrain that bodily enfolds me'. After all: 'It is by borrowing from the world's structure that the universe of truth and of thought is constructed for us.' He tells us, quoting Merleau-Ponty.

I have found in Abram's work the most profound metaphor for structuring time. He assumes that, if we accept the quote above, a time that makes sense will come from the perceivable landscape. The horizon itself can be our structuring metaphor. As we walk towards the horizon it discloses our future, just beyond our reach and yet very much part of our present. As we walk, we can direct our attention to other things we cannot see, to the inside of our bodies, our feet, the ground. The ground under our feet is in a very real sense our past. Layer upon layer of 'stuff' that supports our present. Thus we have our living present, past and future in the now of the world. We find the ground for our conceptual abstraction of time.

---

[109] In *The Spell of the Sensuous*, 1996. Vintage Books.

We can now walk time. Abram says that the past and the future are not elsewhere. 'They are not autonomous dimensions independent of the encompassing present in which we dwell.' These dimensions are instead: 'The very depths of this living place, the hidden depth of its distances and the concealed depth on which we stand.' Here Abram makes the ecological point that linear time functions to eclipse the earth from our awareness, thus enabling us to destroy it. I want to make the existential point that only when time and space are brought together into a harmonious experiential field that connects us to our body and the earth, will we be able to find the peace of mind that we keep searching for in our smartphones.

Furthermore, the harmonious experiential field need not be just with the body and the earth. It may also be with action.[110] We can be in service to a given action. We can act with quality of attention, with precision consciousness towards it. Not in a personal way, like a waiter might seek to build relationship with a customer, but in an impersonal way, like a waiter who attends to all details of the meal because it is demanded by the job he does. We can learn to treat each action as if it were alive, and give it the quality of deep attention that any part of the soul world deserves. James Hillman calls this the new heroic where we learn to give: 'ritual attention to all, not just the altar of self'.

The re-unification of time and body

Where do we start the re-unification? Imagine that a tree perceives you as you take a walk – what does it see? Walk as if the earth feels you – what does it feel? We have talked about the idea of cohering in the 'otherness' of the earth. We have also talked about how we find ourselves in this diversity, rather than by looking in the mirror. All the practices for making the most of our time in the previous chapter point to ways of finding coherence in the world. Meditating on time as a daily practice for developing a healthy sense of time might be the most radical ecological action we can take. Even if ecology is not our concern, meditation is also a way to find the kind of peace of mind that clock time living and the management of time can never give us.

---

[110] James Hillman suggests this idea in *Kinds of Power*, 1995. Currency Doubleday.

When I talk about a faulty, or flawed, sense of time, I mean it literally. Our ability to perceive reality is faulty. Perception is never entirely a bottom up process; it always has an element of interpretation, or top-down processing.[111] We live with the false belief that we see the world as it is. It is more accurate to say that we see the world as we are. Conventional wisdom tells us that we can trust what we see, hear and feel as a true representation of the world. Research in cognitive psychology says that to talk about unconscious awareness is not a contradiction in terms. The field of implicit learning contains substantive evidence that we have a zombie within that acts in the world, without our conscious awareness. What we perceive consciously is a version of the world that, by the time it gets into consciousness, has already been filtered through our individual beliefs, needs, and wants. We sample our experience unconsciously, and categorise it as negative, positive or neutral. We have a tendency to let into conscious awareness only what positively reinforces our view of the world. We reject (by not seeing, hearing or feeling) that which challenges it, and ignore what is neutral.

In other words, by the time we see a tree, for example, we have already made a judgement – is it friend or foe? So we perceive the tree not as it is, but as what we think it is. A London GP sees hundreds of patients who present classic non-specific symptoms associated with acute stress, but her patients consistently argue with her and say they are not stressed, and that they are coping just fine. Faulty perception is this 'denial, the refusal to see how you risk your health, your relationships, and the happiness of those around you'[112] by living only in clock time. The refusal to see is not a conscious act. We actually do not see or perceive the experiences or events that are counter to our belief system. We feel exhausted and unhappy, we breathe polluted air, create piles of rubbish the world cannot dispose of, yet we keep telling ourselves that all is well and that we are coping well. There is a huge gap between the beliefs we espouse, and the actions we embody.

---

[111] See *Hare Brain and Tortoise Mind – why intelligence increases when you think less* by Guy Claxton, 1997. Fourth State. It offers a detailed treatment of the nature of thinking and the cognitive unconscious.
[112] Alison Pearson – *Daily Mail*, April 24, 2003.

5. A philosophy of time

A simple psychological subliminal experiment illustrates this.[113] The results show that we can select interview candidates on the basis of being shown, just below conscious awareness, a picture of a candidate and the word GOOD next to it. Imagine you do an experiment to help me understand decision-making. I ask you to look at a screen, which you perceive as blank, but which shows the picture I just described. I then show you 2 resumes, which are almost identical, and ask you to choose the best-qualified candidate. You choose the one in the picture, and then tell me your rationale for the selection. You have a rationale. You are convinced of it, but the results actually show that what determines the choice of candidate is the picture that was shown below awareness. So, you act on information you are not consciously aware of having perceived. We can even recognise a numerical pattern, use that pattern, and not accept that there is a pattern even when we are told and shown what the pattern is. This means we are shown evidence of what we have actually done, but refuse to accept it as valid because our consciousness is unable to grasp the unconscious pattern.

This point bears repeating. We perceive (see, hear, feel, touch, smell) much more information than we are consciously aware of. What we become conscious of is an already interpreted version of reality that has been filtered through our beliefs, wants, needs, and expectations. More importantly, we act on information that we do not consciously perceive, and when we are made aware of our actions we deny the reality of evidence in favour of keeping our beliefs unchanged.

By definition we cannot perceive how that which we cannot bring into consciousness influences us. If we don't see it, it does not exist. It is possible for students to train a teacher to stay in one side of the room, just by smiling when the teacher walks to one side of the room and looking down to the floor when the teacher walks down to the opposite side of the room. But the teacher is not consciously aware that this learning has taken place. A placebo can reduce pain, but only if your doctor does not tell you that you are receiving a sugar pill. Anxiety will make those with bulimia eat more, but only if they do not

---

[113] Reported in Claxton (see footnote 11).

know what the source of the anxiety is.

As soon as you tell the teacher what he is responding to, he can choose not to respond to the smiles anymore. If you tell the patient that the pill is a placebo, it will not work. If you show the bulimics the sentence that was flashed below conscious awareness – mum is leaving the child – they now know where the anxiety comes from and they eat the same amount as the non-eating disorder group. Once we consciously perceive something we have a chance to choose not to respond to the stimulus, but firstly we have to accept the erroneous nature of our belief that our perception is accurate.

If our perceptual system is by its nature prescriptive and not descriptive – and it is – then it would be wise for us not to always trust what we perceive. We must learn to be more humble about what we think we know. It is possible to re-train our perception, to clean the lenses of perception, to see a little more of reality each day. We do this by developing a practice of lived time. What happens otherwise is that we just tune out what we don't want to hear. Then we live in a world that keeps confirming our beliefs, not because there is no evidence against them, but because our faulty perception stops us from noticing what is there. Living in clock time is like this. The problem is made worse by the fact that conventional wisdom says that we are right in making the intellect our master, that what we know consciously is all we know. Research shows us that we could do worse than learn to perceive the zombie within. It has much more complex information about time, our body and the earth than our conscious mind will ever know. Our aim in life should be, as Jean Liedloff says: 'to make the intellect a competent servant instead of an incompetent master'.

The reunification of time with our body comes from a re-evaluation of the nature of perception. We accept that by the time we notice the world we have already imposed a structure. Research tells us that coins look bigger to hungry children. Experimental data also tells us that when presented with a big container and a small container both weighing the same, we will always think that the bigger one is heavier. If we accept that our self-deception is not just a psychological but also a physical construct we will learn not to deceive ourselves so much, but only when we are able to train our perception to attend to what is, rather than creating that which we believe. This is what will lead us to develop a healthier relationship to time, one that begins to give us genuine choice – a kind of choice that uses 'the competent servant' well. If we become more conscious of what we actually perceive, we are more able to see the habits of body, speech and mind that lead us to act as we do. We develop less of a need to tell justifying stories to make ourselves feel good. This may lead us to make wiser choices with regard to our lifestyle in the present moment.

Something else that conspires against our ability to bring together time and our body in a living present is our slavery to production. Galbraith[114] defines conventional wisdom as: 'ideas which are esteemed for their acceptability'. We associate 'truth with convenience', and in the realm of ideas familiarity breeds acceptability rather than contempt. We will accept as true whatever matches our beliefs, and when hearing what we believe we feel reassured. We accept certain things as true just because we think they should be true, although there may not be support for them in current experience. Conventional wisdom is more often than not out of date. It is made up of beliefs that at one time reflected current events, but do not do so any longer. A lot of data has to accumulate to overthrow conventional wisdom, and those people who challenge it are rarely liked or rewarded in our society.

Galbraith argues that we function with regard to production from outdated conventional wisdom. Our sense that we must produce more and more, and that production is an end in itself stems from a past when poverty made production a worthy activity as it helped create security and reduce inequality. Once a society has clothes, shelter, and food members of the society begin to want other things. We start to want public services. Public services do not so easily lend themselves to an economic model of private production. Yet today we see the production of public services as less worthy of pursuit than private sector products. We are too busy following an ancient conventional wisdom that tells us that products that meet urgent needs are more important than 'luxuries' like street cleaners. Current reality, however, is not one where we are producing for urgent needs

---

[114] In *The Affluent Society* by J. K. Galbraith, 1998. Penguin.

anymore. Keynes divides human needs into 2 categories. Firstly: 'those needs which are absolute in the sense that we feel them whatever the situation of our fellow human beings may be.' and secondly: 'those which are relative only in that their satisfaction lifts us above, makes us feel superior to, our fellows'. Our affluent society has, for the most part, met absolute needs in its members, but our slavery to production is built almost exclusively on a misinterpretation of relative needs as absolute needs.

Conventional wisdom says that we produce to meet absolute needs. We produce to meet the a priori needs of people. People need food, so we produce food, people want clothes, we produce clothes. However, people also want a third classic car for their collection, so we produce that too. We can all see the leap from absolute needs to relative needs in this list. In itself, Galbraith does not see this as problematic. We may not be clear as to what counts as relative and what counts as absolute, but we could build a society on the basis of meeting needs. This works as long as the needs are genuinely a priori. If we can show that our needs are actually created by the process of production, and do not exist independently of the production process, then we have a problem. One way we create need is by 'keeping up with the Jones'; we see what others have and we want it. This is not an a priori or absolute need. We want a higher standard of living, we want more comfort, but we forget that comparatives never make good targets. They keep us wanting more.

Look at the purpose of advertising and sales. These are clear examples of processes that are connected with production, and the sole purpose of which is to create demand for product. You must advertise to create interest in a product. So, if you are spending huge amounts of money in want formation then you cannot argue that the purpose of production is to fulfil need. If you are not fulfilling independently determined wants or needs, why put so much emphasis on producing more and on doing so efficiently?

Our economic system depends on us forgetting the reality of want creation. If we perceive the reality we might make choices that are detrimental to the longevity of the economic system we depend on. For today, says Galbraith, it is society that serves the economy, and not the other way around. In our inability to see the discrepancy between reality and conventional wisdom we have a striking example of faulty perception. Galbraith tells us that we are just like the genuinely humanitarian man who a long time ago was convinced of the dire shortage of hospital facilities in his local town. The humanitarian continues to: 'importune the passers by for money for more beds and refuses to notice that the town doctor is deftly knocking over pedestrians with his car to keep up the occupancy'.[115]

The fact that needs can be created so easily tells us that they are not either absolute or urgent. A hungry person does not need to be told he wants food. Advertising is only effective with: 'those who are so far removed from physical want that they do not already know what they want.'[116] We can be easily manipulated because we lack clear perception of the difference between what is wanted to make us feel superior to others, and what is wanted to meet a genuine physical need. We have lost our ability to perceive the difference. Clock time living as well as the economy depends for its survival on this faulty perception. We think we have to keep breaking up and re-sequencing tasks to maximise efficiency, because we accept the conventional wisdom that production and efficiency in production are inherently good. This leads us to generally not attempt to consume, work, and do less. After all, we feel the urgency in our workplaces and at home, to be efficient at any cost in order to produce more. Unquestioningly we accept that this is necessary – and it is a courageous person that dares to ask: 'why do I need to produce more?'

Galbraith believes that if production creates wants and thus the need to produce more, it becomes possible to argue with equal force that: 'happiness could be as effectively advanced by inefficiency in want creation as by efficiency in production'. There is little point in producing goods of little urgency if life is made intolerable in the process. Galbraith warns us of the dangers inherent in our refusal to develop a clear perception of reality: 'Among the many models of the good society, no one has urged the squirrel wheel. Moreover, the wheel is not one that revolves with perfect smoothness.' Galbraith remarks that aside from the squirrel wheel's doubtful cultural charms,

---

[115] Ibid. Page 129.
[116] Ibid. Page 135

it also has serious structural flaws that may perhaps one day cause us embarrassment. If the process of satisfying the wants creates them, then the person who pushes for the value of production to fulfil these wants is: 'precisely in the position of the onlooker who applauds the efforts of the squirrel to keep abreast of the wheel that is propelled by his own efforts'.

The squirrel wheel as a model for a good society is what underlines life in clock time. An effect of this model that should already be embarrassing us, if we stopped for long enough to notice, is the social imbalance created by our slavery to production. Our private wealth, argues Galbraith, is the cause of our public poverty. The supply of public services suffers because we keep accumulating unnecessary goods. The more goods we accumulate the more we need public services to support them. The more we have the more we throw away, and if: 'appropriate sanitation is not provided, the counterpart of increasing opulence will be deepening filth'. We need a balance between private wealth and public services, and this is exactly what we do not have in our affluent societies today.

We have lost this balance in our pursuit of efficiency at any cost. We do not see what is right in front of our eyes. The human costs of efficiency are huge, and if we are making these sacrifices in order to produce gadgetry we do not need then the sacrifices are pointless. Efficiency need not be our only criterion if we look beyond clock time and beyond accumulating product. If we keep efficiency as our only success criterion, then we need to be aware of the following economic truth we also fail to recognise. Luttwak's law[117] states that if capital is assigned capably to whatever earns the biggest profits, then: 'there is none to spare for institutions that do unprofitable things, because of felt moral obligations or moralistic pretensions, professional ethics or professional conceits, high ideals or mere habit.' We might improve the economic performance of our hospitals by turning them into profit-maximising entities, but we will at the same time: 'deform or even pervert their essential content.'[118] The tension between care

---

[117] In *Turbo Capitalism – winners and losers in the global economy* by Edward Luttwak, 1999. Harper Collins.
[118] Ibid. Page 254.

and efficiency is at the heart of our relationship to time. Caring takes time, whilst efficiency uses time.

James Hillman warns us that care can only be judged by how well it meets the absolute needs of the people who receive it and not by how: 'efficient, fast, frictionless and fault-free' it might be made to be. He goes even further. Hillman says that because every exchange always underpins a relationship, in order to get the most while giving the least is inherently: 'unjust, unethical, antisocial, abusive, perhaps evil. Yet predatory commerce (the free market as it is euphemistically called) operates regularly on the principle of "get most pay the least"'. Even if we do not share his views on the free-market, we may stop and wonder about the wisdom of applying the economic model to our public services in the way we currently do.

There is more to justifying human action than how profitable we can get it to be. If we apply the test of the 4 questions for correct action that we explored in the last chapter, then efficiency can be put in a human context that need not lead us to destroy all that is worthwhile about human life. We first have to notice that we are justifying all action in the name of profit and efficiency, and then we need to perceive that a final purpose that is about more for less carries ethical implications. Clock time keeps us running just fast enough not to notice.

In our search for a time that makes sense perception plays a key role. In order to develop authentic choice we must first see that we have little choice. We must first see that there is so much that we do not see. Perception is theory-laden, and we tend to seek for confirmation of our theories. This works well from an efficiency point of view as we can get things done quickly. To find peace of mind in the re-unification of our body with time and the world we must re-educate our faulty perception through practice. As we do that, we may begin to see our utter dependency on production, we may start to realise that society is creating certain non a priori wants, we may start to see the difference between relative and absolute need, and we may start to wonder how our lives could improve if we consumed a little less, or focused on the quality of each moment a little more.

Clock time has served us well, and has helped us to produce efficiently enough to meet our absolute needs, and many of our relative needs. If we clean the lens of our perception through a practice of lived time, we may start to see that the usefulness of clock time living has reached its limit. If we keep being slaves to producing efficiently, and continue to extend the use of the metaphor of time as money to all human enterprise we will destroy all that gives our life meaning.

We will trade efficiency for the false promise of having a few years before we die reconnecting with all that we gave up for the sake of an efficiency we did not need. As James Redfield reminds us[119]: 'We are certainly learning enough to manipulate this New World for our own benefit, so why not work to raise our standard of living?' He points out we did this four centuries ago, and then continues: 'We shook off the feeling of being lost by taking matters into our own hands, by focusing on conquering the earth and using its resources to better our situation.' He points out that we completely lost ourselves when we created a secular security and produced economic security to replace the spiritual sanctuary we had given up: 'Working to establish a more comfortable style of survival has grown to feel complete in and of itself as a reason to live. We have forgotten that we still don't know what we are surviving for.' Expanding our understanding of time to mean more than the clock and efficiency may help us re-connect with what we are surviving for.

Achievement is about so much more than the efficient production of goods, but clock time living does not allow us to stop the squirrel wheel for long enough to notice and learn. Instead we cling to the false perception that efficiency in clock time will give us what we need. We already have what we need. We just need to learn to see it.

Growth is more than just 'more-thinking'

If the road to achievement in clock time is efficiency, then the proof of it lies in growth. We think about growth purely in terms of what we have called here more-thinking. Growth is accumulation, capacity for consumption, better, big, and even bigger. The direction of growth in our clock time life is always up. In order to achieve we must do more and be more. In this way, the unlimited capacity machine can be created.

---

[119] *The Celestine Prophecy* by James Redfield, 1993. Warner Books.

5. A philosophy of time

In a philosophy of time that makes sense, we need to develop a less adolescent view of growth as proof of what we have achieved in our life. If we can do this then we can measure up against other criteria of success, that are not about more-thinking. We can define achievement as so much more than just the accumulation of new toys.

James Hillman sets himself the task of filling in the shadow side of growth. Previous chapters have explored the consequences of not looking beyond the measures of success of clock time. Here I am going to flesh out the notion of a mature version of growth and how it can help us relate to time differently. Imagine what your life choices would be like if your criteria for growth included some of the notions I will briefly explore below. James Hillman goes as far as saying that our view of growth is often child-like. Growth, in his view, is about more than an upward progression. He proposes 5 new elements[120] that can help us work with growth in a more mature fashion. Growth can be about:

- **Deepening** – a downward direction to growth that can be equated to the roots of a plant that are needed in order for it to have an upward direction. In our life, deepening is about: 'staying with what is happening, staying in the mess. Staying power. This could translate into staying with the organisation and in the job.' Our ability to stay with the mess and work with it is a kind of growth, one that we are pretty poor at when living in clock time. This kind of growth can be called growth of the soul. 'As in a garden or a marriage, deepening brings ugly twisted things out of the soil. It's a work in the dirt'. Clock time gives us little time for this kind of work. It even devalues it as not efficient.

- **Intensification** – not in the sense of making the earth produce more and more, but in the sense that poetic language: 'intensifies by packing lots of implications and references into the small space of a word or a phrase. A poem miniaturises'. The purpose of intensification in clock time is efficiency. For Hillman, the purpose of a mature notion of growth should

[120] In Kinds of Power – A guide to its intelligent uses by James Hillman, 1995. Currency Doubleday.

include intensification for the purpose of complexity, meaning and beauty. A practice of lived time allows us to develop a sense of intensification of each moment as a moment packed with layers of meaning.

- **Shedding** – this includes: 'not just letting go of non-essentials for the sake of renewal', as is the case with the snake shedding its skin. It also includes the radical shedding that is less obviously for a good purpose. Shedding where: 'the very essence of one's organized life is suddenly under fire or swamped. Like a natural catastrophe'. Our ability to handle this kind of radical shedding well is compromised in clock time. We do not see this as part of a notion of growth, and yet it is the very essence of what will help us be successful in life. Our ability to let go of all: 'those identities to which we are so unquestioningly attached' makes us not be fearful of loss and therefore able to take risks. Thinking of shedding as an ability to develop can help us die well and live well.

- **Repetition** – 'is fundamental, not only to machines; it is the fundamental method in both ritual and the arts. It shows the soul's pleasure in practice, in polishing, in precision'. Hillman views repetition as necessary to growth, not for efficiency's sake but for its own sake. If we learn to view repetition as: 'the essence of craft' and as 'the way that things become beautiful' we grow as human beings and nourish our soul. Hillman points out that disinterested repetition is very much part of the rituals of the east, and wonders if it is because they value repetition in this way that they develop such high quality products. We already mentioned the importance of repetition as a meditation in time in the previous chapter.

- **Emptying** – the way in which: 'the empty moment originates the shape of things to come'. We talked about absences in the previous chapter and their value. The way in which: 'music is the result of specifically spaced and timed moments of silence', so achievement in life is the result of specifically spaced moments of emptiness. Our focus then is not to view these empty moments as waste to be eliminated for the sake of efficiency, but as rests that are necessary to our ability to live well. If we measure our achievements by the empty moments of our life in clock time, we cannot be said to be very successful.

Growth as a proof of achievement need not be about more-thinking. It can be about a mature notion of growth that helps us live a life of quality rather than quantity. Hillman's shadow side of growth starts to give us a vocabulary to define success and achievement independent of the measures of clock time. It helps us create a life where time is associated with service to the world, with giving oneself over to an action, with doing right by the action at hand and not with mere efficient shortcuts.

'Measuring' quality

Clock time living has taught us how to measure quantity and efficiency well. However, in this book I have talked about developing a healthy sense of time that is connected to quality. This is a quality of perception and of attention that can be learnt through aesthetic appreciation as a practice, amongst other practices. We may need some guidance to help us know quality when we see it. I offer Wabi-Sabi[121] as a structure to discern quality. Leonard Koren wrote a little book called 'Wabi-Sabi for artists, designers, poets and philosophers' in which he describes the principles of Wabi-Sabi.

Wabi-Sabi describes a way of seeing beauty. It gives us criteria for beauty that encapsulate the difference between clock time and lived time. If clock time sees beauty in the mass-produced, then lived time sees beauty in the one-off and unique. To develop a healthy

---

[121] What follows is my understanding of a book written by an architect who never built anything, and got side-tracked by Japanese culture instead. The concept of Wabi-Sabi is complex not just complicated. I apologise in advance if my analysis breaks up its integrity in any way. I have found it useful to give me another way to appreciate beauty that goes beyond a clock time definition of beauty. *Wabi-Sabi – for artists, designers, poets and philosophers* by Leonard Koren, 1994. Stonebridge Press.

time sense, then, we need to reconnect with a definition of beauty that incorporates the imperfection of real life. The aesthetic ideals of Wabi-Sabi are just such a thing.

Wabi-Sabi is associated with Zen. It is sometimes defined as the Zen of things. It emphasises perceptual insight, beyond intellectual conception. Because of this it is said that the essence of Wabi-Sabi can only be transmitted through lived experience and not through words: 'those who know don't say, those who say don't know'. This has meant that the concept is fuzzy and complex even for the Japanese. Leonard Koren wrote a book that describes the concept because he has a healthy sense of time. He tells us: ' if the ability to create the Wabi-Sabi aesthetic is to be preserved, some guideposts need to be placed for future generations'.

To be submerged in the experience of a Zen monastery for years to absorb meaning is only a reality for the very few. These few words may only be the start of a lifetime of practice for you, and I do not intend the word to replace the experience. In my learning of this philosophy, I am more able to measure beauty in a way that grounds me more each day to the messy imperfect beauty of nature. Something that leaves a feeling of satisfaction in my heart, rather than the distasteful sickly feeling I experience when I think of 20-year old women conforming to a disembodied perfectionist ideal of beauty by injecting botox, a poison, into their bodies.

Koren says that the closest English word to Wabi-Sabi is 'rustic'. The origin of the word came from the hermits and ascetics who lived in isolation and poverty. This way of life came to be associated with opportunities for spiritual richness. It offered attention to the minor details of everyday life, and insights into the often-ignored aspects of nature. As this change of value happened: 'unprepossessing simplicity took on a new meaning as the basis for a new, pure beauty'. What are the differences between our way of seeing beauty in things, and the Wabi-Sabi way? Koren provides us with a table that compares them side-by-side:

5. A philosophy of time

Our Way	The Wabi-Sabi Way
Public domain	Private domain
Implies logic and rationality	Implies intuition
Absolute	Relative
Looks for universal and prototypical solutions	Personal and idiosyncratic solutions
Mass-produced and modular	One of a kind and variable
Has faith in progress	There is no progress
Future oriented	Present oriented
Believes in the control of nature	Nature is fundamentally uncontrollable
Romanticises technology	Romanticises Nature
People adapt to machines	People adapt to Nature
Geometric organisation of form	Organic organisation of form
Metaphor: the box	Metaphor: the bowl
Man-made materials	Natural materials
Slick	Crude
Needs maintenance	Accommodates degradation
Solicits reduction of sensory information	Solicits expansion of sensory information
Intolerant of ambiguity and contradictions	Comfortable with both
Light and bright	Dark and dim
Everlasting	To everything there is a season

This list sums up in a few words the way that we measure beauty from the perspective of clock time, and how beauty can be measured from lived time. But our way promises control forever, so the Wabi-Sabi way is just not perfect enough from a clock time perspective. Denial is definitely not a river in Egypt, Honey! Our way does not reflect real life, which is why we have to keep running to keep the reality away from our perception for long enough that we think that we are running towards The Answer. One of the sad facts of the reality we are running away from is that one in five women: 'defeated by the prospect of juggling work and life, now choose work.'[122] A reality that may be reported as affecting women only, but that has serious implications for the family as a whole. Choosing work over life is not Wabi-Sabi. It is distorted perception.

The tea ceremony is Wabi-Sabi. I remember when I attended one in Japan. I was very much in the mindset of our way and could not understand the point in going to a simple shed-like structure, where I could barely stand up and which was dark and dingy, only to take hours to drink a liquid I found quite unpleasant. Please forgive the ignorance of this description, but I offer it to help you see that we have to educate our attention to see beyond the obvious ways our culture measures beauty. Since that first impression, I have significantly reviewed my position. To this day, years after, when I recall the experience I am filled by a sense of calmness and reverence that I cannot explain. I remember little detail (except for disliking the tea so much) and yet I have a strong memory of the feeling of the occasion, of coming out of the tea-room feeling strangely at peace with myself and my world.

The Wabi-Sabi way can be a guide for how to choose a life where time makes sense. It offers a comprehensive aesthetic system. It looks at the nature of existence, spirituality, our state of mind, our behaviours and the look and feel of material things in the world. We can look at these 5 things through exploring 5 questions from a Wabi-Sabi viewpoint. As you read Koren's list overleaf[123], keep your attention on how choosing to answer these questions in the Wabi-Sabi way can give you peace of mind today.

---

[122] Alison Pearson – *Daily Mail*, April 24, 2003.
[123] Ibid. Page 25

5. A philosophy of time

The Wabi-Sabi Universe	
Metaphysics: What is the universe like?	Things are either devolving towards, or evolving from nothingness. The universe is in constant motion away from or towards potential.
Values: What are the lessons from the universe?	Truth comes from the observation of nature – things are impermanent, imperfect and incomplete. Greatness exists in the inconspicuous and overlooked details – this means you have to slow down, be patient and look closely. Beauty can be coaxed out of ugliness – we see ugliness only because we have not attended deeply enough to find the beauty in all things.
State of mind: How do we feel about what we know?	Accept the inevitable – appreciate the 'evanescence of life'. Appreciate: 'the physical forces and deep structures that underlie our everyday world'.
Morality: Knowing what we know, how should we act?	Get rid of all that is unnecessary – find a balance between the pleasure we get from things and the pleasure we get from freedom from things. Focus on the intrinsic and ignore the material hierarchy – be humble and remember that value is not attached to cost.

Material Things: What objects express our understanding of the universe, or create that understanding in others?	Objects that suggest natural processes – they age and die. Irregular – as they keep a record of life. A bowl that might have broken and been lovingly but imperfectly repaired, for example. Intimate – 'They beckon – get close, touch, relate.' Unpretentious – understated and unassuming, but with presence. Appreciated in contact and use, never put away in a museum. Earthy – usually made from material not far away from its original condition. Can feel rough and unrefined. Murky – not defined, colours blurred, soft. Simple – nothingness is the ultimate simplicity. As in the tea ceremony: fetch water, gather firewood, boil water, make tea and serve it to others. Pares down to essence but doesn't remove the poetry. Keep the quality that: 'compels us to look at something over and over again'. The quality of taking time with things.

I urge you to go to the original source book. I think it a remarkable guide to a healthy sense of time. Each of the questions in the previous table can help us make decisions about the quality of our temporal lifestyle, and each bullet point is a lifetime's work for those of us who are emerging from the slavery of the clock. Focusing on the intrinsic and ignoring the material may help us discover a way to stop being seduced by the shopping mall. And more pragmatically, it may guide us to buy quality that is not defined by the latest fashion fad, thereby saving us much money in the long run!

The key to quality is to give it time. We may then learn the value of staring, and of silence, and of taking time to think. We are to some extent caught in a double bind. This is why we keep going along the same path. It requires courage to be that person who blows the whistle on conventional wisdom. We can choose to keep on the same path, appeasing our conscience with training, and complaining about how our efforts to find work-life balance are just not showing results. A few see beyond the surface of the conflicting demands of today's workplace, and make choices that are rationalised as wrong by conventional wisdom. If you negate the value of anything that challenges your world-view, you will always live in a world where you are right, even when you are wrong.

Reversing conventional wisdom – a way to lived time

> *This being human is like a guesthouse, every morning a new arrival – a joy, a depression, a meanness; some momentary awareness comes as an unexpected visitor. Welcome and entertain them all. Treat each guest honourably. The dark thought, the shame, the malice; meet them at the door laughing and invite them in. Be grateful for whoever comes.*
> Rumi [124]

---

[124] Rumi. Excerpt from 'This being human; Poems and stories by Rumi'. CD published by RGM Ltd., 1998. www.egnet.co.uk/clients/music/rgm.html.

Conventional wisdom gives us general guides to making life decisions. It tells us that most of the time certain things hold true such as most of the time efficiency is good. If we take conventional wisdom as a guide it will generally helps us. The problem comes when the guide becomes a rule without exceptions, for example when we say efficiency is *always* good. When we find a rule of thumb that works we tend to over-apply it. The very thing that once helped us progress becomes limiting when applied without question to all we do. I believe clock time is an example of this. It helped us once, it is now no longer helping us, but we have become incapable of looking beyond it. Conventional wisdom tells us that clock time is *always* good, and this book is a challenge to that 'always'.

If we want our lives to change, we must make time to question what seems self-evident in our life path. Sometimes what we think of as bad can contain some good. Life beyond clock time is about learning to work with this apparent paradox. We have surfaced a number of paradoxes in these pages. We explored how inefficiency can give us lived time and meaning, how discomfort can be a guide to well-being, and how it is sometimes good to aim to have less rather than work more.

An article in the *Financial Times*[125] looks at people who made the lifestyle choice to work as little as possible. It focuses on people who: 'turn their backs on what they see as a culture of too much work and too little pay', and decide to just work less. These people are living beyond the clock. They question the conventional wisdom that to work hard is good: 'From the first day at school we are told to work hard. But Why? Why? Why?' The article goes on to talk about these 'rare creatures' who choose to work less in a world: 'obsessed with productivity and competition'. These rare creatures are: 'neither retired, nor ill, nor among the millions of people half-heartedly trying to engineer a better work-life balance, or attempting to downshift'. These people are: 'cheerfully, proudly, bone-idle by choice'. The article speaks of the social stigma attached to choosing 'laziness'. The stigma is obvious from the tone of the article; these rare creatures are mocked and talked about in a derogatory tone – implying we would

---

[125] 'In an idle world', *Financial Times* May 3/4, 2003.

have to be at best slightly eccentric to choose to work less. One of the people interviewed for the article says that once work was deemed a necessary requirement for an honest livelihood, and: 'happiness was derived from leisure, but now it seems that work is the aim of life. The world would be a much better place if people were lazier'.

This article encourages me even though I am unhappy with its tone. For the *Financial Times* to carry an article that attempts to challenge the conventional wisdom that laziness is always bad may be an indication that, as a society, we are starting to become conscious of the limits of a life in clock time.

If we get into the habit of always and gently questioning self-evident truths we may find a way to life beyond the clock. Is this always a bad thing? Is that always a good thing? Through this discipline we might get a glimpse of deep truth. Nils Bohr said that there are two types of truths; superficial truths and deep truths: 'In a superficial truth, the opposite is false. In a deep truth, the opposite is also true.'[126] In a letter, Robert Dilts tells me that beauty and ugliness are deep truths. We know that there is great beauty in the world, and we know that there is ugliness. These are like two sides of the same coin, light and dark. The candle is dark at its core, and yet gives light when it burns, but the light also casts a shadow. Deep truths are about a 'both-and' way of thinking rather than an 'either-or' way of thinking. Efficiency is both good and bad, so is comfort, and so is work. It is important that we develop the ability to see beyond superficial truths to allow us to choose with fuller information. What are the limits of that which seems self-evidently good? When is it good to do something that seems to be bad? These are all questions to help us connect with the deep truth of lived time.

And in conclusion – Just stop

In order to connect with lived time we need to find a way to STOP. Maybe retreat centres and business schools are one way in which we can stop in a socially acceptable way. We go to those places and find them valuable when they give us a way to stop and enter lived time.

---

[126] Quoted in a personal email by Robert Dilts, September 14, 2001.

We may well believe that the higher effectiveness and confidence we feel is due to the subject we go there to learn, but it may just be that the change is due to having had the opportunity to stop and perceive time in a different way. Perhaps it would be a lot cheaper for employers to give employees time to have a life outside of work rather than send them on expensive training courses. In my own research, I am now turning my attention to using the practices of lived time as a way into working practices that incorporate a mature notion of growth as a measure for success. Through the practices of lived time we may develop working practices that require us, and reward us, for bringing 'ugly twisted things out of the soil', the inconsistencies of clock time. We might learn to talk about being of service to our work rather than about being personally effective and efficient. Lived time may give us peace of mind through self-other balance, if not work-life balance.

The quest for a healthy sense of time ends when we see that we do not have to change what we do. We only have to change how we do it, and as we change the 'how' and not the 'what', we find that we have to do less, but what we do has gained a brightness and meaning it did not have before. A practice of lived time can give us a lifestyle change that is more sustainable than the accelerated de-contextualized ways to change we are offered in clock time. Just commit to the practice and you will find at least one negative consequence of clock time reversed. Luttwak calls this negative consequence: 'the loss of personal authenticity'.

In accepting 'empty form as substance' as a way to make profit; for example, buying a plain cotton T-shirt and paying over the odds for it because it has the name of a designer, we have become accustomed to a kind of lying. Luttwak tells us that we lie all day at the office in order to sell goods or services, and then our lying continues outside office hours so that we can network more effectively at social gatherings as we search for business. He concludes that the lying: 'then persists even at home by sheer habit, until finally reaching the point of lying to oneself'. This soul-destroying process is encouraged by clock time in its pursuit for efficiency.

We enter into stylised conversations that objectify people, what we have called the I-It mode of being. Lutwak[127] argues that we deliberately choose to lose our personal authenticity because we are too scared of the alternative: 'For most people, a wilful retreat from consciousness into a sleepwalker's existence of play-acting one role after another is actually the best remaining option.' And for our leaders such as: 'tycoons, top corporate chiefs, leading politicians and other high achievers, it is the best prescription for success...' This is because to think of greatest principles or: 'simply of true personal desires – as opposed to impressing other people – would only spoil their performance.' A practice of lived time will bring us to questions of ultimate purpose, and will stop us sleepwalking. What is also true is that our performance, as understood by the world of clock time, will certainly be spoiled. Maybe this is one of the paradoxes that we have to explore; bad performance may sometimes be good. If we work with this paradox, if we work at holding seemingly conflicting opposites together, we may find peace of mind today and a way into soulful working and living. Society needs us to expand our notion of time as more than money if it is to move beyond unsustainable definitions of achievement, and if it is to deal with the complex and paradoxical nature of a life with depth, a life with meaningful relationships to the earth and other people.

We are after all: 'lived by powers that we pretend to understand.'[128] Our intellect cannot grasp the consequences of our actions fully. All we can do is attend to the world and be humbled by its immensity if we want to belong to it. Our attempts to control the world through the clock have given us much more inner disquiet than we ever predicted. And to seek inner quiet through yet more attempts to control ourselves and our lives seems analogous to telling that proverbial hamster that it will find rest if only it can keep turning that wheel a little bit faster each day.

---

[127] *Turbo-Capitalism: Winners and Losers in the Global Economy* by E Luttwak, 1999. Harper Collins.
[128] Excerpt from poem 'In Memory of Ernst Toller' by W.H. Auden. Originally published in *Another Time* (1940).

A summary of the book

*Once upon a time there was
Lived time and free time to meet when the cows go grazing,
off time, our time...
Then ticktockman arrived on the scene
And gave us meetings.*

*We learnt to do clock time
We then learnt to fit lived time to clock time
And then came the rush
And time became money*

*We fitted more and more events into our clock hours
Now if we want to make money
And we need to, to buy time
We must fit even more into those self-same hours*

*Enter time urgency
We rush, we rush and we rush
Trying to get to where?
We forget that clock time was once only a good idea*

*We now live to find ways
To control it, as it controls us
And become clock time addicts instead
Why?*

*If our focus is on exercising control over those 24 hours
Over those 7days, over that month and that year,
Then we may never have to stop and ask:
How would I now live if I trashed that 'good' idea?*

*What would I do next?
I would have to stop running towards my future*

I would have to feel the loneliness, the hurt the pain
Of knowing that I run for nothing

Of knowing that
No matter how fast I run
I'm troubled by a future in which I know I will die
And troubled by a life I cannot schedule but can only live

Well at least I now know
I can't control life, but I can control time
And I just have to keep running
To get myself back to Once upon a time...

APPENDIX

A MEDITATION PRACTICE TO FIND TIME BY REV. ANDREW HUNTER

In this 24/7 society, time is something that many say is at a premium. But with inappropriate use of time often comes illness, and many illnesses today are stress related. When we're stressed we tend to ignore our bodies, or drive ourselves too hard. In the process it isn't just our physical well-being that suffers; our mental, emotional and spiritual well-being suffer also, and perhaps most noticeably, the quality of our relationships and life in general begin to go out of balance.

So what's to be done? Well, without fuss or the need to study lots of skills and techniques, regular meditation often provides the answer, though many initially retort with, "I DON'T HAVE ENOUGH TIME." Paradoxically, regular meditation quite naturally allows us to use our time with greater ease. It really DOES help us to reduce, or respond more effectively to stress, *and* improve the quality of our lives and relationships. It really can be that simple. And practised regularly, meditation ushers in so many benefits in many areas of our lives – better health, better quality of relationships, more peace and calm, reduction in abusive behaviour; the list is endless.

So too are the kinds of meditation. There are many, many different approaches to meditation – from the simple – where we go into a meditative state as we stand in wonder at a sunrise or sunset, marvel at the breaking of the waves on the shore, walk in awe in a scent-filled pine forest, or take in the beauty of a colourful flower garden.

It can be as simple a process as lighting a candle and focussing your attention on the flame, or lighting incense – or closing your eyes and letting your mind wander to a place of fond good memory – perhaps a delightful beach scene or a favourite landscape.

Meditation can also be as complex as you want to make it with monks taking up to 20 years to learn the art. Some prefer transcendental approaches, with the repetition of a mantra, which is usually a sacred word, phrase or sound. Others believe that true meditation is only about becoming skilled in finding the stillness within, achieved through observing the Self. Yet others aim to achieve it through quietening the internal thought process, but as the mind is a naturally recurring thinker, that perhaps is rather difficult for most.

Ultimately whether you learn by attending classes, a workshop, a meditation retreat, through a book or perhaps a CD, trust yourself to find a way that works for you. Whichever form you eventually take as your main way, meditation will prove a turning point for you, when life takes on a new meaning and your practice gently guides you to greater well-being and a better way of living.

Research shows that people with many medical conditions respond favourably to meditation. It works really well for those who have high blood pressure, bronchial asthma and headaches. Meditation has also provided excellent relief to those with persistent worry and anxiety, the kind of people who get muscular tension especially in the back and neck. For those who feel tired all the time, meditation has given them more energy, more stamina and has helped those suffering from insomnia to get to sleep, and what's even better, to have improved sleep. It's helped people combat addictions, and allowed them to become less dependent on alcohol, drugs and cigarettes, though in the case of cigarettes it can take a year of regular meditation to witness lasting beneficial results. Meditation has helped many people deal successfully with irritability and depression, and it has helped many of them become more intuitive.

Each person's experience of meditation is unique, and the benefits each derives will vary greatly. It works where it is needed – often with surprising results. It is so important to enter each meditation without condition, or to get into comparing your experience with that of other peoples', or with a previous meditation you have had. Simply allow it to work and see what it can do for you.

Regular meditators often become more quiet, more peaceful, and physically relaxed; their capacity to be effective at work greatly enhanced. People have reported that they have become more open, trusting, less defensive, less irritable and critical, more in touch with and able to express their feelings, they have better self-esteem and confidence. It has enhanced peoples' creativity and productivity.

Meditation often brings about changes in our attitude to ourselves. It helps us be more accepting, loving and peaceful. Meditation can help get rid of our bad habits of self-criticism and self-limiting ways of thinking thereby allowing us to be more self-aware, self-responsible, self-assertive, and to develop a quiet inner strength.

For some people meditation is simply about sitting and relaxing. With so many people finding their lives out of balance, with all the different demands made on them, they don't seem to have time to just be, to stand and stare or to sit. They don't find time to go within to that still, small place inside which, when we connect with it, becomes such a powerhouse of peace, love and wisdom. Many people are so obsessed fretting over the past and worrying about the future that they seldom stop to listen to today. Meditation is a good way of taking time out, allowing yourself to tune into and appreciate the moment. It is about being in touch with your inner world, about reaching the quiet centre of yourself. It's about finding an inner stillness, a way of seeking quiet moments, regularly, systematically and which brings about many benefits.

Meditation is often linked closely to Buddhism, which has indeed defined many stages of meditation that are practised in order to achieve the ultimate level of purifying and stilling the mind, clearing it of all thoughts and mental images. You may be familiar with yoga, and if so will be aware of yoga as meditation, very much in the Hindu *hatha* yoga tradition of practising postures to gain physical and mental control, and *bhakti* yoga, a focussing of the mind. These practices are much the same as Christian and spiritual meditations in which the meditator focuses his or her attention upon an aspect of their god, or universal energy or life force. For those of you living in the western world you will probably be aware that meditation in Christian communities has long been a tradition in convents and monasteries. So, we are not dealing with something that is new, untried or untested.

A simple yet effective form of meditation
Here is a form that you can practise if you have only a few moments spare. Avoid doing this when driving, cycling, using equipment or doing anything else that needs your attention.

This technique is borrowed from age-old yogic and T'ai Chi practices, and allows you to slow down your brain waves to take you into a deep state of relaxation. Why not try it now?

For ease of use make an audio file of the instructions, but do ensure that the recording lasts ten to fifteen minutes, and speak slowly leaving little gaps where you see [ ] :

Make sure you are seated in a comfortable position on a chair, and have the next ten to fifteen minutes completely free of interruptions. [ ]

Have your legs placed, uncrossed on the floor and your arms held loosely by your side or on your lap. [ ]

Know that what you are about to do is perfectly safe. [ ]

Begin by drawing in through the nose a long deep breath [ ] At the end of the breath, gently begin to breathe out through the nose, but allow the out breath to be longer than the in breath. [ ]

Then once more draw in through the nose a long deep breath. [ ] At the end of the breath, gently begin to breathe out through the nose, but allow the out breath to be longer than the in breath. [ ]

And once more, draw in through the nose a long deep breath. [ ] At the end of the breath, gently begin to breathe out through the nose, but allow the out breath to be longer than the in breath. [ ]

Just continue for the next 2 –3 minutes, focussing on the in breath and the out breath, always allowing the out breath to be longer than the in breath. [ ]

And now, very gently, place the tip of your tongue on the roof of your mouth behind your two front teeth and keep it there for at least ten minutes, noticing any sensations as you do so. Simply observe the sensations: [ ] there may be tingling in the face, numbness around the nose, itchiness, a tightening of the jaws, a heaviness in neck and limbs, warmth. [ ] Remember you are perfectly safe.

If you need to swallow do so, and return the tongue to the roof of the mouth.

[after 10 minutes]

And now it is time to gently release your tongue from the roof of your mouth and return it naturally to its resting position. [ ]

Become aware of the rest of your body, [ ] and slowly begin to draw in longer deep breaths, this time ensuring that the in breaths are longer and deeper than the out breaths. [ ]

Begin to move your fingers and toes, your arms and legs, your buttocks, feel your back on your chair [ ] really become aware of your body and then, when you feel ready, with one more deep breath, gently open your eyes.

Sip a warm glass of water, and then gently go about your business.

So, how did you get on? If you felt any tingling sensations, or lightness in the body, or even gentle tightness around the face then this is perfectly normal. The more you practise this technique, then cumulatively the more powerful and beneficial it becomes for you. Without effort, you can begin to notice many beneficial changes in your life.

So there you have a simple yet highly beneficial technique that you can use any time you have five minutes to spare, or whilst waiting for an appointment.

There are many great books and tapes on meditation. Andrew Hunter has produced a CD specifically for beginners called "Beginner's Guide to meditation". This includes a 20-minute guided meditation. Please visit www.andrewhunter.eu/meditation if you want to buy his CD.

BIBLIOGRAPHY

Abram, David. *The Spell of the Sensuous: Perception and Language in a More-than-human World*. New York: Pantheon, 1996. Print.

Arnold, Johann Christoph. *Drained: Stories of People Who Wanted More*. Farmington, PA: Plough Pub. House, 1999. Print.

Bstan-'dzin-rgya-mtsho, and Howard C. Cutler. *The Art of Happiness: A Handbook for Living*. New York: Riverhead, 1998. Print.

Burch, Mark A. *Simplicity: Notes, Stories and Exercises for Developing Unimaginable Wealth*. Gabriola Island, BC: New Society, 1995. Print.

Chödrön, Pema. *When Things Fall Apart: Heart Advice for Difficult Times*. Boston: Shambhala, 2000. Print.

Church, Margaret. *Time and Reality; Studies in Contemporary Fiction*. Chapel Hill: University of North Carolina, 1963. Print.

Ciulla, Joanne B. *The Working Life: The Promise and Betrayal of Modern Work*. New York: Times, 2000. Print.

Claxton, Guy. *Hare Brain, Tortoise Mind: How Intelligence Increases When You Think Less*. [New York]: HarperCollins, 2000. Print.

Claxton, Guy. *Wise Up: The Challenge of Lifelong Learning*. New York, NY: Bloomsbury, 1999. Print.

"The Continuum Concept: In Search of Happiness Lost EBook Download." *The Continuum Concept: In Search of Happiness Lost* Free EBook. Web. 11 June 2012. <http://free-ebook-download.org/The-Continuum-Concept:-In-Search-of-Happiness-Lost.html>.

Covey, Stephen R., A. Roger. Merrill, and Rebecca R. Merrill. *First Things First: To Live, to Love, to Learn, to Leave a Legacy*. New York: Simon & Schuster, 1994. Print.

Dreyfus, H. L., S. E. Dreyfus, and Athanasiou. *Mind over Machine: The Power of Human Intuition and Expertise in the Era of the Computer*. Oxford : Basil Blackwell, 1989. Print.

Dreyfus, Hubert L. *What Computers Still Can't Do: A Critique of Artificial Reason*. Cambridge Mass: MIT, 1994. Print.

Hafiz, Daniel Landinsky, and H. Wilberforce Clarke. *I Heard God Laughing: Renderings of Hafiz*. Walnut Creek, CA: Sufism Reoriented, 1996. Print.

Flaherty, Michael G. *A Watched Pot: How We Experience Time*. New York: New York UP, 1999. Print.

Galbraith, John Kenneth. *The Affluent Society*. Boston, MA: Houghton Mifflin, 1958. Print.

Gleick, James. *Faster: The Acceleration of Just About Everything*. New York: Pantheon, 1999. Print.

Griffiths, Jay. *A Sideways Look at Time*. New York: Jeremy P. Tarcher/Putnam, 2002. Print.

Heintel, Peter. *Against Acceleration: Stopping and Thinking for a New Time Culture*. 1999. Print.

Hillman, James. *Kinds of Power: A Guide to Its Intelligent Uses*. New York: Currency Doubleday, 1995. Print.

Hirshfield, Jane, Komachi Ono, and Shikibu Izumi. *The Ink Dark Moon: Love Poems*. New York: Vintage, 1990. Print.

Hochschild, Arlie Russell. *The Time Bind: When Work Becomes Home and Home Becomes Work*. New York: Metropolitan, 1997. Print.

Husserl, Edmund, and John Barnett. Brough. *On the Phenomenology of the Consciousness of Internal Time: (1893 - 1917)*. Dordrecht: Kluwer, 1991. Print.

Jackson, John Brinckerhoff. *A Sense of Place, a Sense of Time*. New Haven: Yale UP, 1994. Print.

Jönsson, Bodil. *Unwinding the Clock: 10 Thoughts on Our Relationship to Time*. New York: Harcourt, 2001. Print.

Johnson, Mark, and George Lakoff. *Metaphor and Communication*. Trier: LAUT, 1982. Print.

Johnson, Mark. *Philosophical Perspectives on Metaphor*. Minneapolis: University of Minnesota, 1981. Print.

Johnson, Mark. *The Body in the Mind*. Chicago: University of Chicago, 1987. Print.

Keyes, Ralph. *Timelock: How Life Got So Hectic and What You Can Do About It*. New York, NY: HarperCollins, 1991. Print.

Koren, Leonard. *Wabi-sabi for Artists, Designers, Poets & Philosophers*. Berkeley, CA: Stone Bridge, 1994. Print.

Lakoff, George, and Mark Johnson. *Metaphors We Live by*. Chicago: University of Chicago, 1980. Print.

Lakoff, George, and Mark Johnson. *Philosophy in the Flesh: The Embodied Mind and Its Challenge to Western Thought*. New York: Basic, 1999. Print.

Le, Guin Ursula Kroeber. *The Earthsea Quartet*. London: Penguin, 1993. Print.

Levine, Robert. *A Geography of Time*. Oxford: Oneworld, 2006. Print.

Luttwak, Edward. *Turbo-capitalism: Winners and Losers in the Global Economy*. New York: HarperCollins Publishers, 1999. Print.

Osborn, Carol. *Enough Is Enough*. New York: New World Library, 1991. Print.

Patten, Brian. *Love Poems*. London: Allen & Unwin, 1981. Print.

Pearson, Alison. *I Don't Know How She Does It: The Life of Kate Reddy, Working Mother : A Novel*. New York: Anchor /Random House, 2003. Print.

Pollack, Robert. *The Missing Moment: How the Unconscious Shapes Modern Science*. Boston: Houghton Mifflin, 1999. Print.

Rechtschaffen, Stephan. *Time Shifting: Creating More Time to Enjoy Your Life*. New York: Main Street, 1997. Print.

Redfield, James. *The Celestine Prophecy: An Adventure*. New York: Warner, 1993. Print.

Richmond, L. *Aging as a Spiritual Practice: A Contemplative Guide to Growing Older and Wiser*. New York: Gotham, 2012. Print.

Richmond, L. *Work as a Spiritual Practice: A Practical Buddhist Approach to Inner Growth and Satisfaction on the Job*. New York: Broadway, 1999. Print.

Salten, Felix, John Galsworthy, Whittaker Chambers, and Kurt Wiese. *Bambi*. New York: Grosset & Dunlap, 1929. Print.

Senge, Peter M. *The Fifth Discipline: The Art and Practice of the Learning Organization*. New York: Doubleday/Currency, 2006. Print.

Sennett, Richard. *The Corrosion of Character*. New York: W. W. Norton, 1998. Print.

Stent, Gunther S. *The Coming of the Golden Age; a View of the End of Progress*. Garden City, NY: Published for the American Museum of Natural History [by] the Natural History, 1969. Print.

Stevens, Chris. *The Alexander Technique*. Optima, 1980. Print.

Sullivan, Anne McCrary. *At the Intersection of Art and Research: The Teaching of Poetry/the Poetry of Teaching*. 1996. Print.

Sullivan, Anne McCrary. *Notes from a Marine Biologist's Daughter: A Collection of Poems*. 1991. Print.

Warner, C. Terry. *Bonds That Make Us Free: Healing Our Relationships, Coming to Ourselves*. [Salt Lake City]: Shadow Mountain, 2001. Print.

Whipp, Richard, Barbara Adam, and Ida Sabelis. 'Making Time Time and Management in Modern Organizations'. Web. <http://www.knovel.com/knovel2/Toc.jsp?BookID=2069>.

Whiteland, David. *Book of Pages*. Manchester: Ringpull, 2000. Print.

Whyte, David. *The Heart Aroused*. London: Industrial Society, 1999. Print.

Wurman, Richard Saul. *Information Anxiety*. Indianapolis: QUE, 2001. Print.

Zulley, Jürgen, and Barbara Knab. *Unsere Innere Uhr: Natürliche Rhythmen Nutzen Und Der Non-Stop-Belastung Entgehen*. Freiburg Im Breisgau. Herder, 2000. Print.